SAP S/4 HANA Sales Certification Questions

By

John Kirk

Copyright Notice

All rights reserved. Do not duplicate or redistribute in any form.
SAP SG is unaffiliated with and does not endorse this Book or its contents. All other trademarks are the sole property of their respective owners.

Table of Contents

Sales Documents 4
Simplifications 15
S/4 HANA Essentials 23
Enterprise Management Execution 26
Billing Process and Customizing 36
Smart Business 46
Basic Functions (customizing) 57
Pricing and condition technique 67
Sales Process 73
Shipping Process and Customizing 80
Availability Check 87
Organizational Structures 93
Cross functional Customizing 99
Master Data 106

Sales Documents

1. Which of the following structure elements a sales document consists of?
   (There are three correct answers to the question)

   (a) Header
   (b) Operations
   (c) Items
   (d) Scheduled Line

Answer: a, c, d

Explanation:

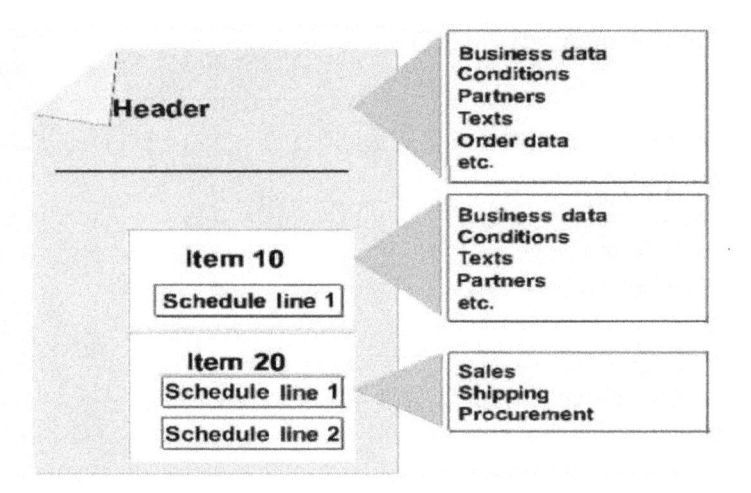

Every sales activity in SAP System is recorded as a sales document. Each business process in the SAP system is represented by a document. For example, a sales document is created when you process a sales order.

The sales document consists of a document header and as many items as required. The document header contains the general data and default values that are valid for the whole document. Each item can contain as many schedule lines as needed. The document items contain data about the goods and services that are ordered by a customer. This data includes material numbers, descriptions, prices, terms of delivery, and payment.

The data for shipping and procurement are displayed in schedule lines. The delivery deadline and order quantity are also shown in schedule lines. Therefore, each line item with delivery requirements must contain at least one schedule line.

2. In which of the following document types the sales price of a material can be found on item level?
   (Only one answer is correct)

   (a) Sales Document Type

(b) Delivery Document Type
(c) Billing Document Type
(d) Shipping Document Type

Answer: a

Explanation:

In SAP we can represent different business processes in sales, shipping, and billing with the following specifically designed document types:

- Sales document types for example inquiries, quotations and standard orders
- Delivery document types for example outbound delivery and returns delivery
- Billing document types for example invoices, credit memos and debit memos

Each document is identified with a unique document number. A match code helps you search for the required document. Each document is assigned an overall status, which reflects the processing status of the document.

The overall status depends on the different status values in the document. These values reflect the processing statuses for the different steps of the sales activity.

3. **Which of the following are the main objectives of creating organizational structures in SAP system?**
   (Only one answer is correct)

   (a) Complex corporate structures
   (b) For processing of data in company codes
   (c) To differ among the different views of sales
   (d) All of the above

Answer: d

Explanation:

The objectives of creating organizational structures in the SAP system are as follows:

- To represent complex corporate structures flexibly
- To adapt to changes in the corporate structure
- To distinguish between views in logistics (such as sales, distribution and purchasing), cost accounting, and financial accounting
- To process data across company code

4. **Which of the following business partners are essential for a sales transaction?**
   (There are two correct answers to the question)

(a) Sold-to-Party
(b) Contact Person
(c) Ship-to Party
(d) Forwarding Agent

Answer: a, c

Explanation:

The essential business partners for a sales transaction are

- Sold-to party
- Ship-to party
- Payer
- Bill-to party

These business partners play various roles in the business process. These roles are known as partner functions. The SAP system provides an entry screen for each type of business partner. When you enter a sales document, you can also enter the ship-to party instead of the sold-to party. The system then determines the sold-to party based on the ship-to party.

The system determines the sold-to party as follows:

- If there is exactly one sold-to party for the ship-to party, the system automatically determines the sold-to-party.
- If there are several possible sold-to parties for the ship-to party, the system displays a selection screen with the possible alternatives.
- If a sold-to party cannot be determined, the system issues an error message in the status bar.
- If you inadvertently enter a ship-to party in the sold-to party field, the system issues a message. The system then continues to process the data as if you had entered the ship-to party in the ship-to party field.

5. Which of the following system checks occur during the determination of the delivering plant?
   (Only one answer is correct)

   (a) Customer Material Information Record
   (b) Customer Master Record
   (c) Material Master Record
   (d) Sales Master Record

Answer: a

Explanation:

Determination of Delivering Plant

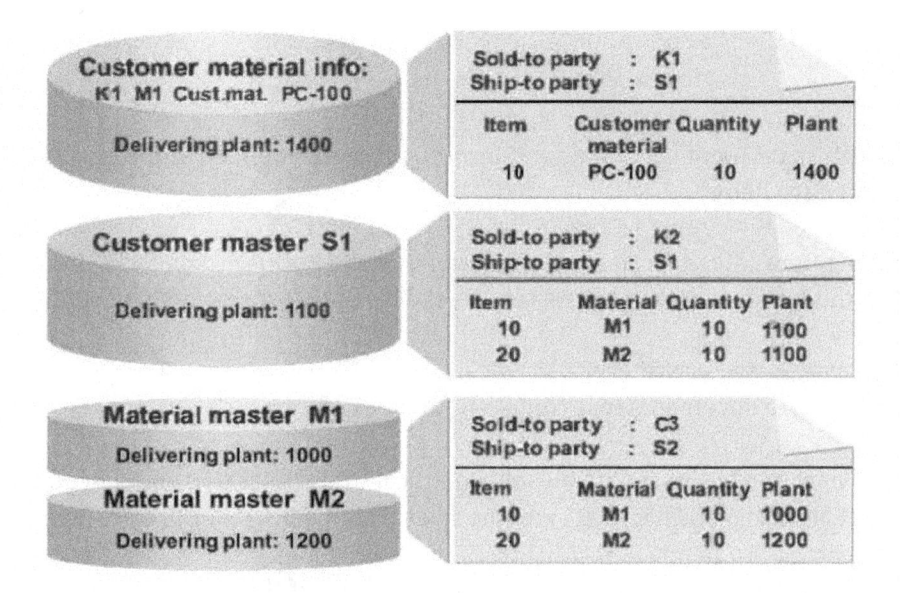

A plant is an integral part of logistics. It takes the role of a delivering plant in sales. When you enter an item to be delivered, the SAP system attempts to determine a delivering plant automatically from the master data. If the search is successful, the results are copied to the document item. Alternatively, you can change this plant manually.

While searching for the delivering plant, the SAP system checks several master data records in the following sequence:

- The system will check whether it can propose a delivering plant based on an entry in the customer-specific material information record.
- If the customer-specific material information record does not contain a plant or if there are no customer-specific material information records, then the system checks the customer master record for the ship-to party.
- If the system does not find the ship-to party, the delivering plant is determined from the material master record.

If there is no plant in the material master record, the system cannot determine a valid plant. If the system cannot determine a valid plant, it cannot determine any other document data, such as the shipping point. Furthermore, no availability check is possible and no delivery can be created.

6. In which of the following level a billing block can be set in a sales document?
   (There are two correct answers to the question)

   (a) Header level
   (b) Item Level
   (c) Scheduled Line level
   (d) Plant Level

Answer: a, b

Explanation:

Business data (such as payment conditions and Incoterms) can be defined at the document header level or for each item.

Customizing for the item category can be decided whether the business data at the item level must differ from the business data at the header level. This option can be defined separately for each item category.

This allows you to create documents that contain both types of items

- Items in which the business data must be identical to the sales document header and
- Items that allow the business data and the sales document header to be different.

7. **Which of the following can be adjusted in the customizing of the sales document type? (There are two correct answers to the question)**

    (a) Billing relevance
    (b) Immediate Delivery
    (c) Increment of Item numbers
    (d) Increment of document numbers

Answer: b, c

Explanation:

In Customizing for the sales document type, you configure the settings that influence the sales process.

Some of these settings are as follows:

- Sales document category
- Delivery and billing blocks
- Document types for deliveries and billing documents

You can also define some default values for the document creation. You can overwrite these values at various levels of the document to match particular procedures such as the delivery date requested by the customer or certain basic requirements for contracts.

In addition, you can activate various checks such as messages about open quotations or outline agreements, searches for customer-specific material information records, or checks for the credit limit. Note that activating checks can affect the system performance.

8. **Which of the following field in the material master records influences the item category determination?**

(Only one answer is correct)

(a) Division
(b) Material Group
(c) Item Category Group
(d) Billing Category

Answer: c

Explanation:

Item Category Determination:

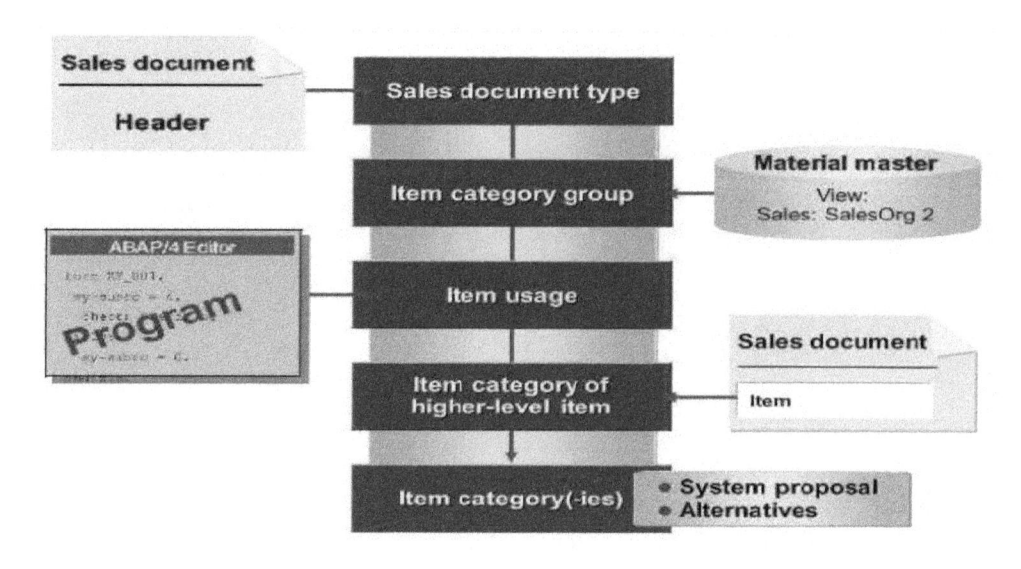

Item categories are assigned to sales document types. The purpose of assigning the item categories are as follows:

- To configure the system so that the system automatically proposes an item category when you create an order.
- To define alternative item categories that users can choose instead of the system default. The assignment of item categories is influenced by the item category group in the material master record.

The item category group allows you to group various materials that have the same function in the sales and distribution processes. If required, you can also define new item category groups. In some cases, the usage for the item is set internally in the program.

For example, the system uses TEXT if you enter an item in the inquiry or quotation by specifying only the item description and not the material number. FREE is used to control free goods items. In the case of a sub-item, the item category of a higher-level item is used.

9. Which of the following functions can be triggered in the scheduled line category?
(There are two correct answers to the question)

(a) Pricing
(b) Transfer of Requirements
(c) Availability Check
(d) Transfer of Billing Documents

Answer: b, c

Explanation:

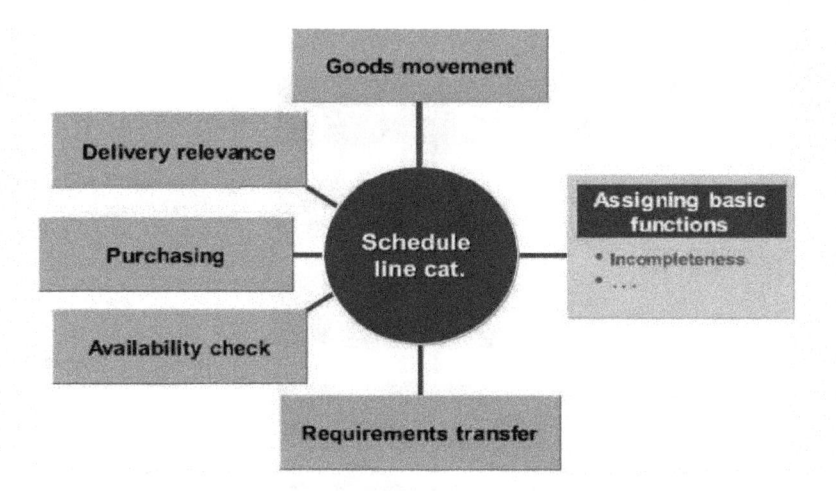

Schedule lines contain delivery dates and material quantities. Schedule lines also contain information about requirement transfer and inventory management. Schedule lines are a prerequisite for delivering materials.

In Customizing for item categories you decide if you want to allow schedule lines for the item. You can assign schedule line categories to each item category. By defining a schedule line category, you determine which schedule lines are actually relevant for delivery. You need to activate the relevant for delivery indicator if you want the goods to be physically delivered.

In the schedule line category, you set the movement type to control the changes in quantities and values that are posted to inventory accounting. Inventory management is responsible for maintaining the movement types. Movement types have been configured for all processes in the SAP standard system.

10. Which of the following is the highest organizational unit in the SAP structure?
(Only one answer is correct)

(a) Company code
(b) Sales Organisation
(c) Distribution channel

(d) Client

Answer: d

Explanation:

- All organizational units within a client correspond to one business unit. Therefore, a client functions as a synonym for the corporate group. A client is an independent technical unit within the SAP system. General data and tables that are used for several organizational structures are stored at this level.
- You can use the company code and business area to represent a group from a financial accounting perspective.
- You must create at least one company code for a client. You can also create several company codes for each client to simultaneously process financial accounting for several independent companies.
- Each company code represents an independent accounting unit. Several company codes can use the same chart of accounts.

11. Which of the following criteria helps in restricting the master records for free goods? (Only one answer is correct)

    (a) Calculation Rule
    (b) Scales
    (c) Minimum Quantity
    (d) All of the above

Answer: d

Explanation:

Free goods are determined by using the condition technique. Free goods are generally regarded as a supplement to the pricing agreement for a material.

You maintain free goods in the master records for sales by using either of the following methods:

- Use a menu entry.
- Go to prices and discounts or surcharges when maintaining the master records.

You can define master records for free goods at any level, such as material, customer/ material, price list category/currency/material or customer hierarchy/material.

You can restrict master records for free goods at one level by specifying the following criteria:

- **Validity period**: The condition is only valid within this period.
- **Minimum quantity**: The condition comes into effect when this quantity has been exceeded.
- **Calculation rule:** The quantity of free goods that a customer receives is based on the calculation rule and the condition that you define.
- **Scales:** When a customer orders a particular quantity of goods, the quantity of free goods is based on the scales and the condition you define.

12. **Which of the following checks can be deactivated in the sales document type for setting up a Cash Sale scenario?**
    (There are two correct answers to the question)

    (a) Open Contracts
    (b) Customer material info records
    (c) Commitment date
    (d) Payment Cards

Answer: c, d

Explanation:

A wide range of checks and functions can be activated in the sales document type. For example, you can activate checking for open contracts or searching for customer material info records. These checks take place during document processing and can affect system performance.

Following checks can be deactivated that you do not need

- Credit Limit
- Purchase Order number
- Commitment date
- Notes on quotation, outline agreements and group contracts
- Product attribute messages
- Payment Cards

13. **Which of the following are the valid key combinations of the master records for material listing?**

(Only one answer is correct)

(a) Customer/Material number
(b) Customer group/material
(c) Customer/Product Hierarchy
(d) All of the above

Answer: d

Explanation:

You want to ensure that your customer receives only specific materials. You enter these materials in the material listing for that customer. The material listing is customized by the condition technique.

The example in the figure indicates that master records have been created with a key combination for the customer and material numbers. This key combination is delivered in the standard system. But you can also define your own key combinations.

Examples:
- Customer group/material
- Customer/product hierarchy

The access sequence for the condition type guarantees that the system searches for valid master records for both the sold-to party and the payer. You define in the sales document type whether the system must check the material listing.

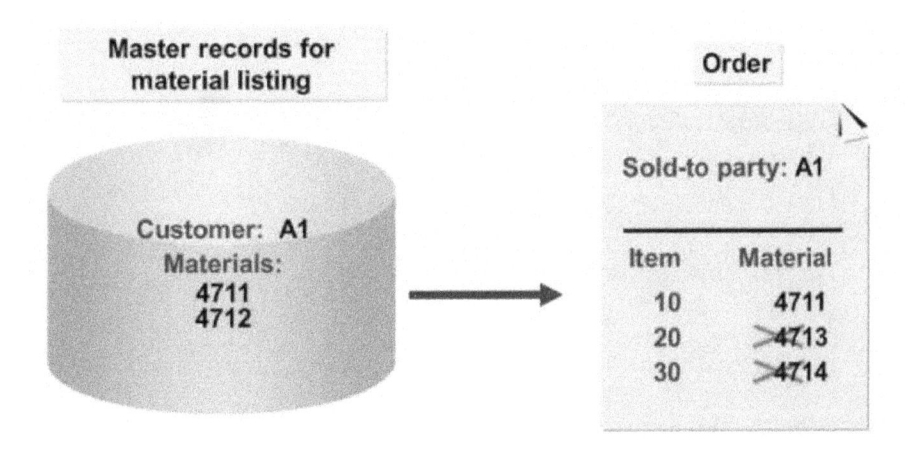

14. **At which of the following levels you can assign the incompletion procedure?**
    (Only one answer is correct)

    (a) Header Level
    (b) Item Level
    (c) Schedule Line Level

(d) All of the above

Answer: d

Explanation:

The incompletion log differentiates between the header, item, and schedule line levels in a sales document.
In each incompletion procedure, you determine which fields are to be checked for completion. You assign incompletion procedures to sales documents to determine the areas of validity. For example, you can assign an incompletion procedure to the sales document header based on the sales document type.
You can assign the incompletion procedure at the following levels:

- The header level by using the sales document type
- The item level by using the item category
- The schedule line level by using the schedule line category

You can also set partner functions. texts, and condition types in pricing as mandatory. If these entries are missing, a note will appear in the incompletion log.

Simplifications

15. Which of the following are the business partners?
    (There are two correct answers to the question)

    (a) Customer
    (b) Vendor
    (c) Personnel
    (d) Agent

Answer: a, b

Explanation:

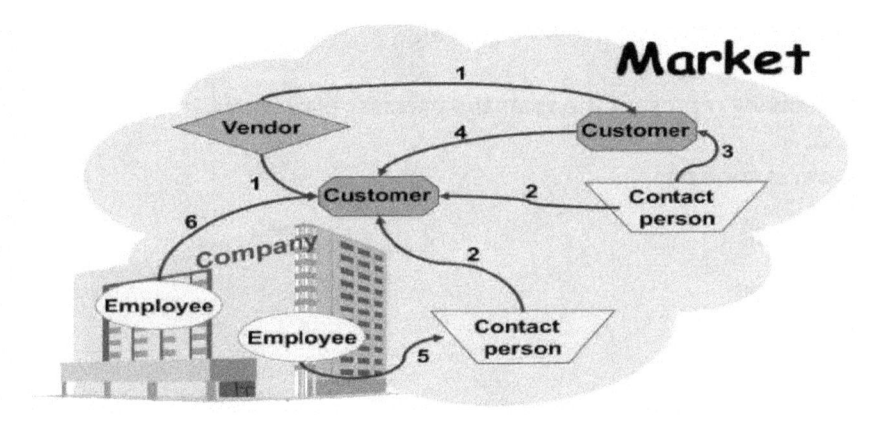

Various business partners exist within the marketplace. These business partners have various business relationships with each other.

Examples of business partners are as follows:
- Customer
- Vendor
- Employee
- Contact person

16. Which of the following partner types are defined in Sales & Distribution application module?
    (There are three correct answers to the question)

    (a) Customer
    (b) Vendor
    (c) Personnel
    (d) Agent

Answer: a, b, c

Explanation:

In the SAP system a partner type represents the business partners in the marketplace. The partner types AP, KU, LI and PE are defined in partner processing for the Sales and Distribution application module.

These partner types are defined as follows:

- AP is used for the contact person.
- KU is used for the customer.
- LI is used for the vendor.
- PE is used for the personnel.

Other partner functions such as O for organizational unit, S for position and A for work center are used in other applications such as Service Management.

17. **Which of the following represent the roles the partners play within the business transaction?**
    (Only one answer is correct)

    (a) Partner Type
    (b) Partner Function
    (c) Business Partner
    (d) Partner Controller

Answer: b

Explanation:

The partner types distinguish between different business partners and the partner functions represent the roles the partners play within the business transaction.

For example, different customers (customer partners) can assume certain roles in a business transaction. The customer who places the order does not necessarily have to be the same customer who receives the goods or the customer who is responsible for paying the invoice.

You can determine the function or functions of particular partners in the sales process by assigning partner functions in the SAP system. One partner can take on several functions.

In the simplest case all partner functions within the customer partner type are assigned to a single business partner. In other words, the same customer is the sold-to party, ship-to party, and payer and bill-to party.

18. **Which of the following assignment key is relevant when partner determination procedure is assigned to partner object Customer Master?**
    (Only one answer is correct)

(a) Account Group
(b) Sales document type
(c) Delivery Type
(d) Shipment Type

Answer: a

Explanation:

Partners appear in the system at various levels such as in the customer master, sales document header and sales document items. You can define your partner determination procedures for each of these levels. In a partner determination procedure, you determine which partner functions must be displayed. You determine areas of validity by assigning procedures.

For example, you use the account group to assign the partner determination procedure for the customer master. The following table lists the relevant assignment keys when partner procedures are assigned to partner objects:

Partner Object	Assignment Key
Customer master	Account group
Sales document header	Sales document type
Sales document item	Item category in sales
Delivery document header	Delivery type
Shipment	Shipment type
Billing header	Billing type
Billing item	Billing type
Sales activities (CAS)	Sales activity type

19. When you create sales documents, business partners are automatically copied from the customer master, and then which of the following partner function is the preferred source for the customer master?
(Only one answer is correct)

(a) Ship-to-Party
(b) Sold-to-Party
(c) Bill-to-Party
(d) Plan-to-Party

Answer: b

Explanation:

Account groups are already defined in the standard SAP system. For example, 0001 is the sold-to Party, 0002 is the ship-to party, and 0003 is the payer. You can create additional account groups if necessary.

When you create sales documents business partners are automatically copied from the customer master. In the process the customer master of the sold-to party is accessed.
Several partner relationships for a sold-to party are stored in the customer master record.

For example, a customer master record for a customer who acts as a ship-to party only (created with account group 0002) requires information that is relevant for shipping. Billing information is not required. Therefore, the corresponding fields are not displayed.

20. Suppose you have various regular suppliers in various regions and you want the system to determine the forwarding agent in the sales document depending on the ship to party then which of the following statement ensures that system determines the correct forwarding agent?
(Only one answer is correct)

   (a) Access the master record of sold to party and then access master record of ship to party
   (b) Access the transactional record of sold to party and then access master record of ship to party
   (c) Access the master record of ship to party and then access the master record of sold to party
   (d) Access the transactional records from the master data and then trigger a workflow to determine the agent

Answer: a

Explanation:

Several partner relationships for a sold-to party are stored in the customer master record. The system can also copy a partner function from other customer master records to create sales document.

Consider an example of indirect partner functions. You have various regular suppliers in various regions. You want the system to determine the forwarding agent in the sales document depending on the ship-to party.

In Customizing, you ensure that the system determines the ship to party by first accessing the master record for the sold-to party. Then the system accesses the master record of the ship-to party to determine the forwarding agent.

You can also use other sources to automatically determine business partners in sales documents. For example, you can use the tables for customer hierarchy (KNVH) contact persons (KNVK) and credit representatives (T024P).

21. Which of the following contracts are frequently used in the service industry?
   (Only one answer is correct)

   (a) Quantity Contract
   (b) General value Contract

(c) Material related value contract
   (d) Rental and maintenance Contract

Answer: d

Explanation:

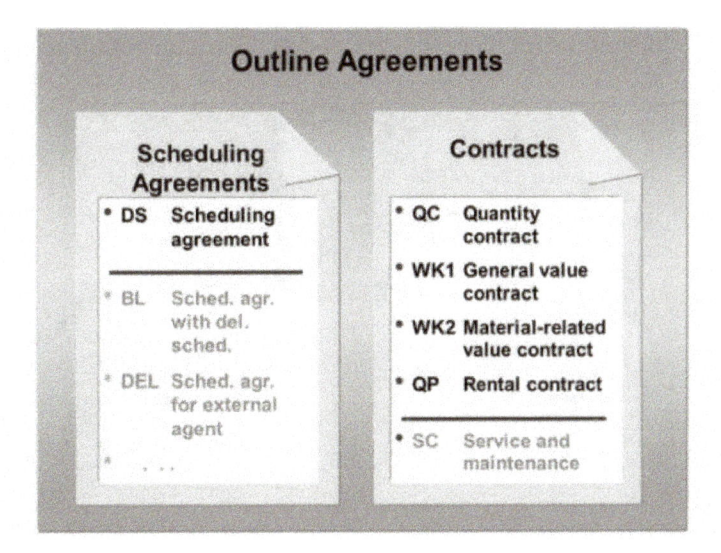

Outline Agreements

Scheduling Agreements
- DS Scheduling agreement
- BL Sched. agr. with del. sched.
- DEL Sched. agr. for external agent

Contracts
- QC Quantity contract
- WK1 General value contract
- WK2 Material-related value contract
- QP Rental contract
- SC Service and maintenance

Outline agreements play an important role in nearly all business processes. Customers and vendors agree on the goods to be provided, based on certain conditions and within a specific period of time. Outline agreements streamline business processes for both partners in a business relationship.

In the SAP system, various sales document types represent outline agreements. These sales document types that can be used directly or copied as templates.

The two main outline agreements are scheduling agreements and contracts. The simplest and most common type of scheduling agreement is represented in the system by the document type DS.

There are two types of contracts: value and quantity.

Contracts can cover both goods and services. Generally, no restrictions apply to the contract forms.

Rental and maintenance contracts are frequently used in the service industry. Maintenance agreements are signed for the products that a customer uses over a long period of time and will need to be serviced periodically.

22. **Which of the following tab pages are available for Create with Reference dialog box while creating sales documents?**
    (Only one answer is correct)

(a) Inquiry
(b) Order
(c) Contract
(d) All of the above

Answer: d

Explanation:

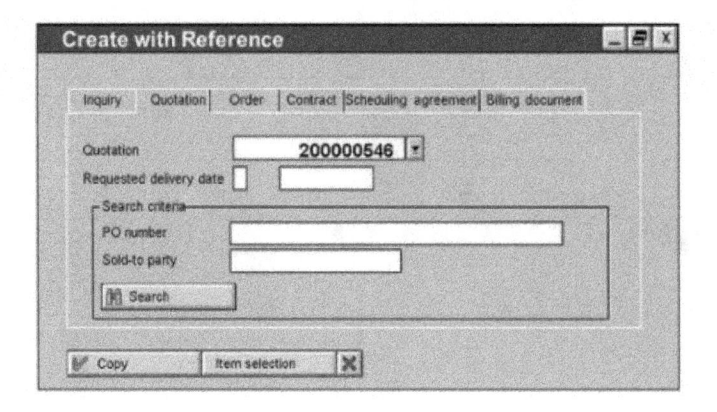

The creation of sales documents with reference to preceding documents helps to build document flows, which in turn describe business processes. Information is transferred from the preceding document to the subsequent document (data flow).

The status of the preceding document is also updated. The document flow provides an overview of the business process and can be analysed. You can create a sales document with reference to a preceding document either from the initial screen or during document processing. You can control the process by using the Create with Reference dialog box.

The dialog box has the following tab pages:

- Inquiry
- Quotation
- Order
- Contract
- Scheduling agreement
- Billing document

The default tab page that appears when you first access the dialog box is determined by the system based on the sales document category and the Mandatory reference field.

23. **Which of the following delivery type system creates automatically when you save the rush order?**
   (Only one answer is correct)

(a) BV
(b) LF
(c) RO
(d) SO

Answer: b

Explanation:

```
        Sales document type
        RO - Rush Order

        Imm. delivery:   X
        Delivery type:   LF
```

RO - Rush Order
Document number: 2973
Sold-to party: C1

Item	Material	Amount
10	M1	10
20	M2	20

LF - Delivery
Document no.: 8000 0070
Sold-to party: C1

Item	Material	Amount
10	M1	10
20	M2	20

Created automatically

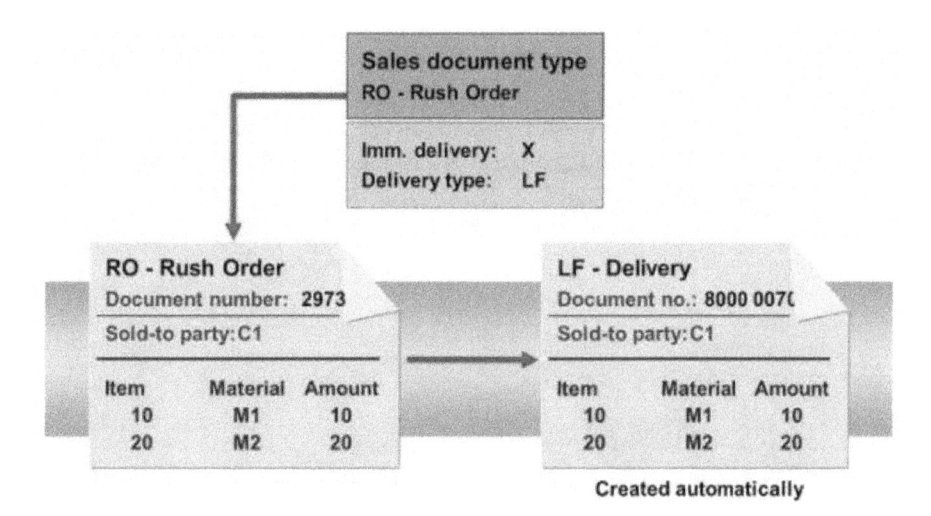

Rush orders and cash sales are sales document types that are used when a sale is made directly from a plant or when customers need to pick up goods immediately from the warehouse.

In the rush order sales document type the immediate delivery switch and the delivery type LF are configured. When you save a rush order, the system automatically creates a delivery of the LF type.

After the goods are withdrawn from the warehouse the picking and posting of goods issue can begin. When you create the billing documents (for example in collective processing) the system prints the invoice papers and sends them to the customer.

24. **Which of the following business relationship exists between Vendor and customer? (Only one answer is correct)**

    (a) Vendor acts as forwarding agent for the customer
    (b) Customer is employed at the company of vendor
    (c) Sold to party and ship to party of both customer and vendor are same
    (d) Each customer is assigned as a vendor

Answer: a

Explanation:

Various business partners exist within the marketplace. These business partners have various business relationships with each other. Examples of business partners are as follows:

- Customer
- Vendor
- Employee
- Contact person

Examples of business relationships are as follows:

Vendor and customer The vendor acts as the forwarding agent for the customer.
Contact person and customer The contact person is employed at the company of the customer.
Contact person and customer The contact person is the consultant of the customer but does not work at the same company.
Customer and customer The sold-to party and ship-to party are not the same.
Employee and contact person Each contact person is assigned a sales employee.

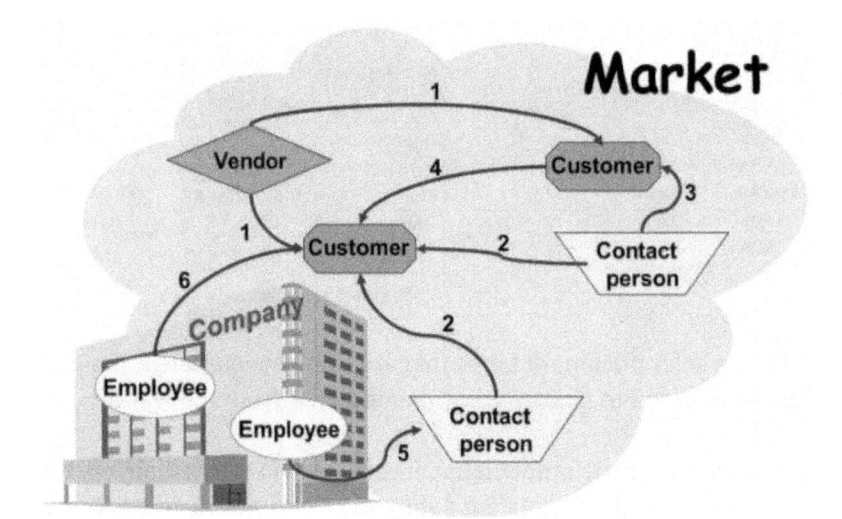

S/4 HANA Essentials

25. Which of the following dimension is a simplification of the user experience?
(Only one answer is correct)

(a) Fiori Concept
(b) Fiori Design
(c) Fiori Technology
(d) Fiori Architecture

Answer: a

Explanation:

SAP Fiori UX is the new face of SAP to business users for ALL lines of business including new solutions on HANA and also native cloud acquisitions such as Success Factors, Ariba, Field glass etc., across devices and deployment options.

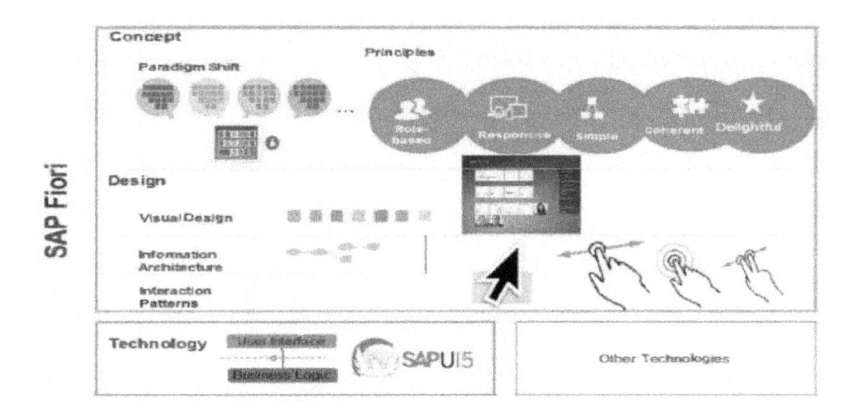

SAP Fiori comes with the three different dimensions:

- Fiori Concept
- Fiori Design
- Fiori Technology

The Fiori concept - fundamentally- is a simplification of the user experience. It reflects a paradigm shift for delivering a holistic and consistent user experience that is centered only on the tasks and activities that matter to the personal needs of the end user. At the core, the Fiori Principles define the overall concept.

26. Which of the following is a single entry point for SAP Business functions?
(Only one answer is correct)

(a) SAP Fiori Launch Pad
(b) SAP Fiori Active Tiles
(c) SAP Fiori Technology

(d) SAP Fiori Dashboard

Answer: a

Explanation:

The latest installment has 300+ apps supporting a large variety of roles in more lines of business, including HR, finance, manufacturing, procurement and sales. The apps offer users the ability to conduct transactions, get insight and take action as well as view factsheets and contextual information.

Enhanced Look and Feel, including:

SAP Fiori Launch pad - a single entry point for SAP business functions - contextual, role-based, personalized, and search enabled.

SAP Fiori Active Tiles - provides the most impactful real-time information and KPIs at a glance

27. **SAP provides which of the following to analyse the critical KPIs in real time?**
    (There are two correct answers to the question)

    (a) Tiles
    (b) Drill down
    (c) Drop boxes
    (d) Themes

Answer: a, b

Explanation:

KPI tiles
- Every value scenario comes with predefined KPI tiles and drill-down configurations. SAP provides 4 standard KPI visualizations. Based on threshold calculations the end user gets alerted as soon as a KPI value becomes critical.
- The end user can freely arrange his KPIs and other tiles based on the Fiori launch pad.

Drill-down
- SAP provides a standard drill-down to analyze critical KPIs in real line. The drilldown configuration can be easily adapted by simple configuration.
- Alternatively, customers can use SAP Lumira or Analysis Path Framework for advanced analytics.

28. **Which of the following are the different Fiori App types?**
    (Only one answer is correct)

    (a) Transactional
    (b) Analytical

(c) Factsheet
(d) All of the above

Answer: d

Explanation:

Transactional:
Task Based Access: Access to tasks like change, create or approve processes with guided navigation.
Analytical
Insights: Visual overview over a complex topic for monitoring or tracking purposes
Factsheet
Search and Explore: view essential information about objects and contextual navigation between related objects

29. **Which org units and master data fields do you need to be able to determine the storage location in the delivery item based on the MALA rule?**
    (There are three correct answers to the question)

    (a) Plant
    (b) Shipping point
    (c) Storage condition on customer master
    (d) Storage condition on material master.

Answer: a, b, d

Explanation:

Specification of the storage location in the delivery document item based on the MALA rule depends on the following criteria:

- Shipping point
- Plant
- Storage conditions

The storage conditions that apply to storage of a material are stored in the material master record. You will find the specification on the tab page Plant data / Warehouse for a material in the field Storage condition.

Enterprise Management Execution

30. Which of the following interconnects all aspects of the value chain in real time to drive business outcomes?
    (Only one answer is correct)

    (a) Digital Core
    (b) Enterprise network
    (c) Big Data
    (d) Enterprise services

Answer: a

Explanation:

Digital Value Network, the digital value network starts with a digital core, which interconnects all aspects of the value network in real-time to drive business outcomes. The digital core gives consumer-product companies the opportunity to re-platform core business processes and brings together business process with analytics in real time.

- Workforce engagement
- Mobility
- Collaboration
- Contingent labor

- Intelligent products
- Embedded software
- Internet of Things
- Solution business
- Digital content

- Workforce engagement
- Assets & Internet of Things
- Supplier collaboration business networks
- Consumer experience omni-channel

- Collaborative R&D
- Supply networks
- Networked procurement
- Solution provider network

- Segment of One
- Omni-channel engagement, sales, and service
- IoT-based engagement

Re-platform core business processes, and bring together business process and analytics in real time to be smarter, faster, and simpler

This enables a smarter, faster and simpler enterprise, which includes connecting every aspect of internal operations, and also enables real-time processes such as the following:

- Workforce engagement to retain and grow existing talent, attracts new talent, and preserve enterprise intelligence with a smarter, engaged workforce.
- Supplier collaboration through business networks to mitigate supply risk, accelerate growth and help ensure global compliance all while maximizing product availability and margins.
- The Internet of Things and Big Data, combining internal, external, social, and sensor data to enable real-time visibility to quantifiable measures of consumer demand and other market dynamics with qualitative measures of consumer sentiment, intent, and behavior.

This entire value chain, including the core, is digitized, and serves as the platform for innovation and business process automation.

31. **Which of the following are the features of SAP S/4 HANA Enterprise Management?**
    (Only one answer is correct)

    (a) Innovative in memory database
    (b) Renewed Applications
    (c) New UI technology
    (d) All of the above

Answer: d

Explanation:

SAP S/4HANA Enterprise Management builds the next-generation business suite

- Innovative in-memory database
- New architecture and data models
- Renewed applications
- New UI technology
- Cloud &on premise deployment Models

SAP S/4HANA is a new product. With SAP S/4HANA, we are building on the success of the SAP Business Suite powered by SAP HANA with a completely new and re-imagined suite.

SAP S/4HANA runs on SAP HANA and provides simplicity (for example, a simplified data model with no indexes, no aggregates and no redundancies) and promotes innovations (for example, open in-memory platform for advanced applications predicting, recommending and simulating).

32. **From a business value perspective SAP S/4 HANA creates the unique opportunities in which of the following ways?**
    (Only one answer is correct)

    (a) Reduction of Data Foot Print
    (b) Easily accessible to deliver new values to the customer
    (c) New User Experience
    (d) Non-disruptive Architecture

Answer: b

Explanation:

Business Value Position from a business value perspective, SAP S/4HANA creates unique opportunities to reinvent business models and drive new revenues in the following ways:

- Enterprises can easily connect to people, devices and business networks to deliver new value to their customers - the Internet of Things and Big Data become accessible to any business.

- Enterprises can dramatically simplify their processes and change them as required to gain new efficiencies - batch processing is no longer required.
- Business users can now get any insight on any data from anywhere in real-time: planning, execution, prediction and simulation - all decisions can be made instantly with the highest-level of granularity for faster business impact.

33. **From an IT value perspective SAP S/4 HANA creates the unique opportunities in which of the following ways?**
    (There are three correct answers to the question)

    (a) Reduction of Data Foot Print
    (b) Easily accessible to deliver new values to the customer
    (c) New User Experience
    (d) Non-disruptive Architecture

Answer: a, c, d

Explanation:

IT Value Proposition

From an IT value perspective, SAP S/4HANA creates unique opportunities to simplify the landscape and reduce Total Cost of Ownership (TCO) with SAP HANA in the following ways:

- The user experience of SAP S/4HANA is natively designed with SAP Fiori UX, offering an integrated and modern usability on any device.
- The architecture of S/4HANA is non-disruptive. That means, Business Suite on premise customers can easily upgrade or fully migrate to the cloud or enable hybrid deployments.
- Enterprises can now significantly reduce their data footprint and work with larger data sets in one system.

34. **The updated data model for SAP S/4 HANA Enterprise management involves which of the following changes?**
    (Only one answer is correct)

    (a) Avoiding Joins
    (b) On- fly- aggregation
    (c) Semantically corrected data
    (d) All of the above

Answer: d

Explanation:

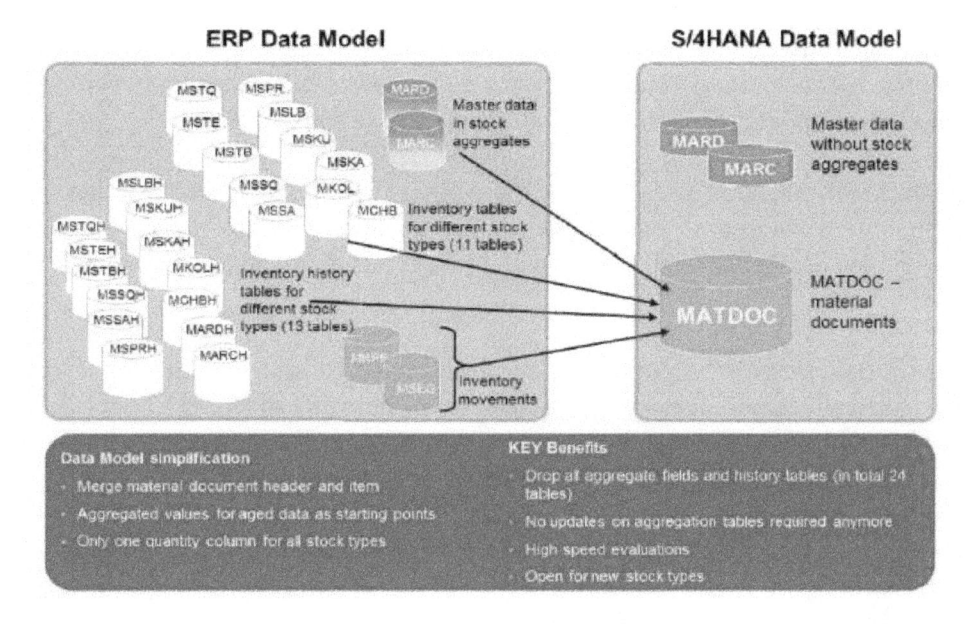

As shown in the figure, Inventory Management - Improvement by Elimination of Aggregates, simplification of the ERP data model of inventory management led to the creation of one document table for material documents (MATDOC). This updated model involved the following changes:

- Merging header and item level (avoiding joins)
- Enabling on-the-fly-aggregation
- Semantically corrected material master data table

Aggregate tables are not deleted physically. The redirect feature (transaction SE11) guides any table access to the new persistency. The reason for this is the compatibility with legacy code (for example, customer code, industries, and so on).

35. SAP S/4 HANA supports which of the following valuation methods?
    (Only one answer is correct)

    (a) S- price
    (b) V-price
    (c) Actual Costing
    (d) All of the above

Answer: d

Explanation:

S/4HANA supports the following valuation methods:

- Standard Price (the so-called S-Price)
- Moving Average Price (the so-called V-Price)
- Actual Costing (which is mandatory in some countries like Brazil)

In S/4HANA, we have a better performance, especially in mass processing, for example, back flush in Repetitive Manufacturing, which is basically due to fewer tables (aggregates) to be booked, especially no updates on cumulative values in the material master.

For S-Price only, the throughput is improved as there are no application locks any longer (parallel updates are supported). Moreover, to enable inventory valuation at actual costs and improved throughputs, you can use Actual Costing (based on Material Ledger) instead of using a moving average price.

Furthermore, the data footprint is reduced. Reporting is no longer based on material ledger tables, which only know material relevant data and cannot provide insights into financial dimensions (for example, no information like profit center, functional area). The new reporting is based on the unified journal entry that combines material and financial data.

36. **Which of the following are the innovations of Material Requirement Planning in terms of its capabilities?**
    (There are two correct answers to the question)

    (a) Real time alerting solution
    (b) Monitoring reports
    (c) Frequent runs
    (d) Reduced Sales Orders

Answer: a, c

Explanation:

Business Challenges
- Improve customer service levels
- Improve inventory accuracy
- Avoid revenue losses due to stock outs

Business Benefits
- Clear visibility across the material flow increases user acceptance and efficiency
- Proactive decision making in response to changing demand
- Flexible tailoring of available capacities and receipts to meet required quantities
- Real time inventory monitoring and automating the creation of procurement proposals

Capabilities
- Real-time alerting based on current stock requirements situation
- System-generated solution proposals
- MRP can run as frequently as required (up to 10x faster)

37. **Sales Order Fulfilment cockpit in S/4 HANA Enterprise management helps the internal sales representative in which of the following ways?**
    (There are two correct answers to the question)

(a) Order creation
(b) Exception handling
(c) Detecting issues earlier
(d) Improved customer satisfaction

Answer: c, d

Explanation:

Order fulfillment cockpit changes the working mode for the internal sales representative. Before S/4HANA Enterprise Management, the main task of the internal sales representatives was order creation and management, without a comprehensive view of the overall order situation or exception handling.

With S/4HANA Enterprise Management, there is now an exception-based working mode to detect issues earlier and improve customer satisfaction by using the Sales Order Fulfillment cockpit.

This change brings business benefits such as a reduction in order-to-cash cycles, as well as outstanding payments, while the service level is increased.

38. Which of the following component is the most widely used industry solution within SAP and used cross industry solutions?
    (Only one answer is correct)

    (a) SAP DIMS
    (b) SAP DIMP
    (c) SAP STC_CONT
    (d) SAP DMIS

Answer: b

Explanation:

Discrete Industries and Mill Products (DIMP) is the most widely-used industry solution within SAP and used cross-industry customers.

The SAP DIMP component adds sector-specific functionality to SAP ERP to satisfy the complex requirements of discrete industries (for example, manufacturing, automotive) and mill industries (for example, metal, wood, paper, textiles, construction materials, and cable sectors).
Therefore, SAP must support these End- to -End Processes via S/4HANA.

Total distribution of DIMP Usage inside and outside of original DIMP Industries (Automotive, Aerospace & Defence, Engineering, Constructions & Operations, Mill Products)

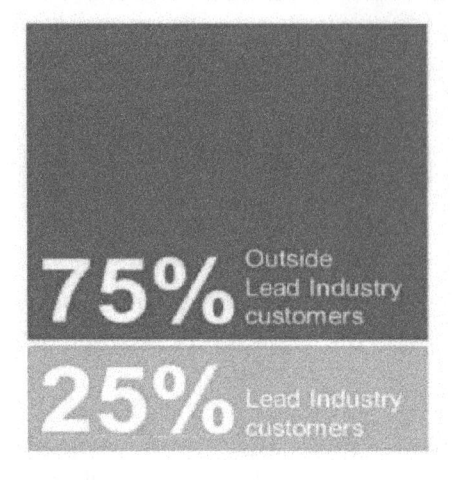

75% Outside Lead Industry customers

25% Lead Industry customers

DIMP is the most widely used industry solution within SAP.

This solution is heavily used by cross industry customers.

Therefore SAP's strategy has to support these End-to-End Processes via S/4HANA.

39. Which of the following are the drawbacks of separating the OLAP and OLTP systems? (Only one answer is correct)

(a) OLAP system does not have the latest data
(b) Lot of redundancy
(c) Cost intensive to synchronize both the systems
(d) All of the above

Answer: d

Explanation:

Modern Enterprise Resource Planning (ERP) systems are challenged by mixed workloads, including OLAP-style queries. For example:

- OLTP-style, such as create sales order, invoice, accounting documents, display customer master data or sales order.
- OLAP-style, such as dunning, available-to-promise, cross selling, operational reporting (list open sales orders).

However, today's data management systems are optimized for daily transactional or analytical workloads, storing their data along rows or columns.

Drawbacks of Separation

The following are some evident drawbacks of a separation:

- The OLAP system does not have the latest data.
- The OLAP system only has a predefined subset of the data.
- The Cost-intensive ETL process has to sync both systems.

- There is a lot of redundancy.
- Different data schemas introduce complexity for applications combining sources.

40. **Which of the following are the benefits of performing S/4 HANA Analytics?**
    (Only one answer is correct)

    (a) Zero Latency of Data
    (b) Uniform
    (c) Extensible
    (d) All of the above

Answer: d

Explanation:

The following are benefits of Performing SAP S/4HANA Analytics:

- Getting real-time analytics back to where it belongs: Into the operational system.
- Operational reporting: Analytics directly on the original transactional data.
- Real-time: Zero latency of data.
- Lightweight modeling and consumption: Modeling and access based on open standards (SQL, MDX, ODATA).
- Extensible: Easily extend SAP's model.
- Uniform: All models across SAP Business Suite are built according to the same guidelines.
- Basis for multiple embedded use cases: ready for embedded analytics.
- Model reuse in analytical applications: Analytical models will be used to build new analytical applications for the Business Suite powered by SAP HANA.

41. **With SAP S/4 HANA, which of the following is supported for real time operational reporting?**
    (Only one answer is correct)

    (a) SAP Core data services
    (b) ABAP Modeling
    (c) SAP Business objects with Analytics
    (d) SAP Lumira

Answer: a

Explanation:

SAP S/4HANA blends transactions and analytics, allowing operational reporting on live transactional data.

With SAP S/4HANA, this concept is supported in the form of SAP Core Data Services for real-time operational reporting. The content is represented as a Virtual Data Model (VDM), which is based on the transactional and master data tables of SAP SAHANA. Core Data Services (CDS views) are developed, maintained and extended in the ABAP layer of the S/4HANA System. The system generated SQL Runtime Views in SAP HANA to actually execute the data read and transformation inside the SAP HANA Database Layer. SAP want to create a Virtual Data Model using Core Data Services (CDS views) as to support (and replace all other standard ABAP-related standard) operational reporting in the context of S/4HANA.

The advantage of this approach is full ABAP-integration, allowing for reuse of existing reporting authorizations, and so on. Also, we can use the analytical engine (embedded BW functionality) to support elaborate hierarchy display. This allows the creation of more use cases for this Virtual Data Model.

SAP S/4HANA Analytics supports not only generic operational OLAP reporting. It also supports scenarios of embedded analytics for hybrid transactional and analytical applications (for example, SAP Embedded BI or SAP Smart Business Cockpits) based on the same models. Read-access for Search or Fact Sheets is also supported when we plan new extractors for EDW staging into SAP BW to create consistency between the models.

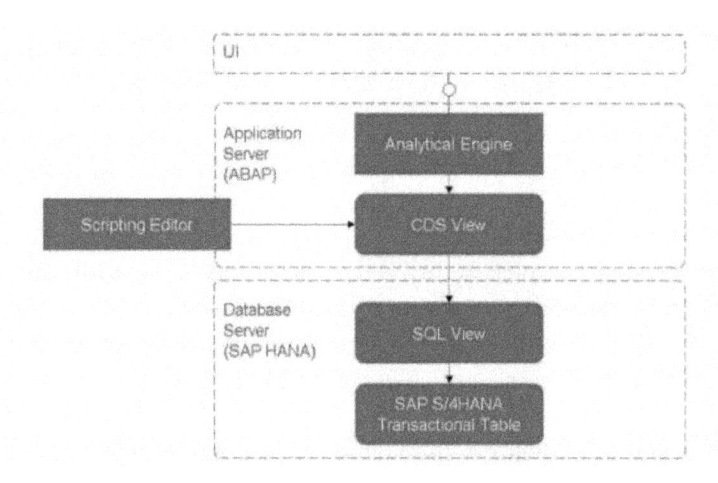

42. **A warehouse management system performs the following functions?**
    (Only one answer is correct)

    (a) Tracking of an item
    (b) Connects to external systems
    (c) Location tracking
    (d) All of the above

Answer: d

Explanation:

Warehouse Management System Functions
A Warehouse Management System performs the following functions:

- Tracks the amount of an item or material that is stored in a warehouse.

- Tracks the location of every storage bin that holds a particular good or material.
- Controls and record all movements of goods and materials in the warehouse.
- Connects to mobile data entry as part of integrated radio frequency solution.
- Connects to specialized external systems (for example, an automated warehouse system) using an interface.

Billing Process and Customizing

43. Billing documents are made up of the following?
(There are two correct answers to the question)

- (a) Header
- (b) Items
- (c) Schedule Line
- (d) Only Items

Answer: a, b

Explanation:

Billing Document Structure

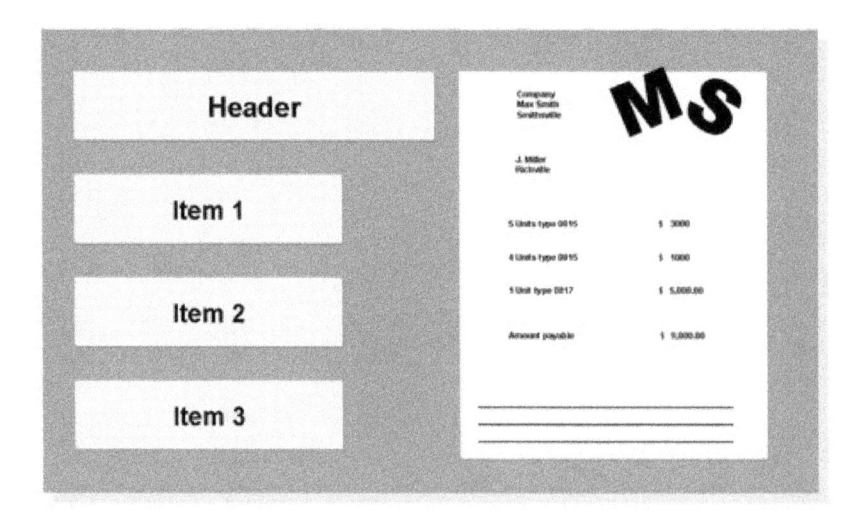

All billing documents have the same structure. They are made up of the header and any number of items.

The header contains the general data that is valid for the entire billing document. This includes:
- Customer number of the payer
- Billing date
- Net value of the entire billing document

The items contain the data relevant for each individual item. This includes:
- Material number
- Billing quantity
- Net value of the individual items

44. In which of the following ways you can create credit and debit memo requests?
(Only one answer is correct)

(a) Without reference to a previous business transaction
(b) With reference to an order
(c) With reference to a billing document
(d) All of the above

Answer: d

Explanation:

You can create credit and debit memos either with reference to credit or debit memo requests (sales documents), or, if your company does not require a release procedure in the case of complaints, directly with reference to a billing document.

You can create credit and debit memo requests:
- Without reference to a previous business transaction
- With reference to an order
- With reference to a billing document

45. Which of the following controls are found at item level?
(Only one answer is correct)

(a) Billing quantity
(b) Reference document
(c) Allocation numbers
(d) Item numbers

Answer: a

Explanation:

The following controls are found at item level:

- Billing quantity: Which quantity should be invoiced - the order or delivery quantity?
- Pricing and exchange rate
- Should pricing, for example, be carried out again or should prices from the order be copied over, and at what exchange rate?
- Updating the quantity and value in the reference document
- Where the conditions in the billing document should be carried over from (for example, copying over shipment costs from the shipment cost document)?

46. Which of the following system uses as a basis for combining the transactions to be billed?
(Only one answer is correct)

(a) Sold-to-party
(b) Billing date
(c) Destination country
(d) All of the above

Answer: d

Explanation:

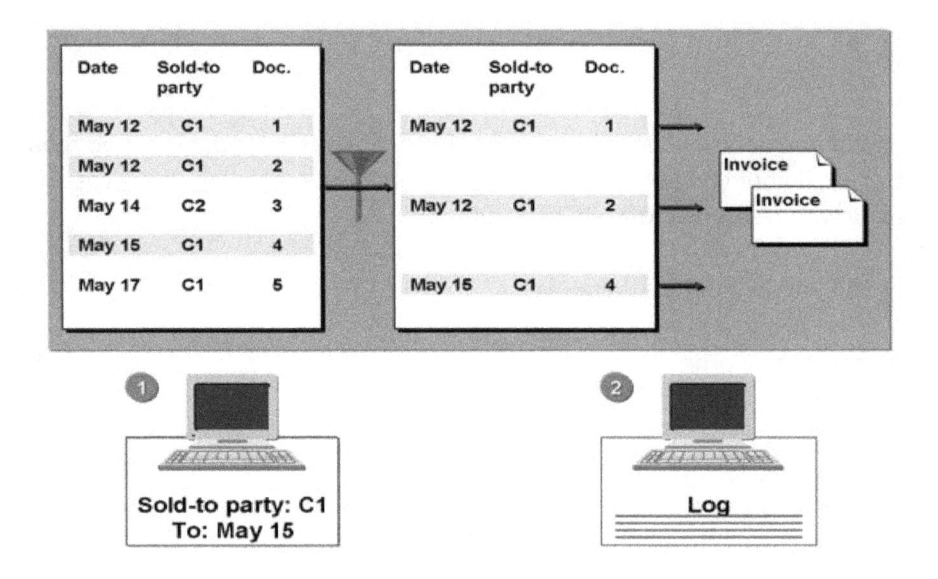

Bill transactions are usually not carried out individually rather it is done by collective billing runs (by goods issue posting, for example)

When working with the billing due list, enter the selection criteria (such as sold-to party, billing date, and destination country). The system uses the selection criteria as a basis for combining the transactions to be billed.

When selecting, you can also decide whether the billing due list should only contain documents that are order-related, delivery-related or both.

47. Suppose you have orders and deliveries not created in the SAP system then which of the following are the mandatory required fields to be maintained in the data records to invoice the external document using the General Billing interface?
(There are two correct answers to the question)

   (a) Customer Master
   (b) Material Master
   (c) Sales Organization
   (d) Price Components

Answer: a, c

Explanation:

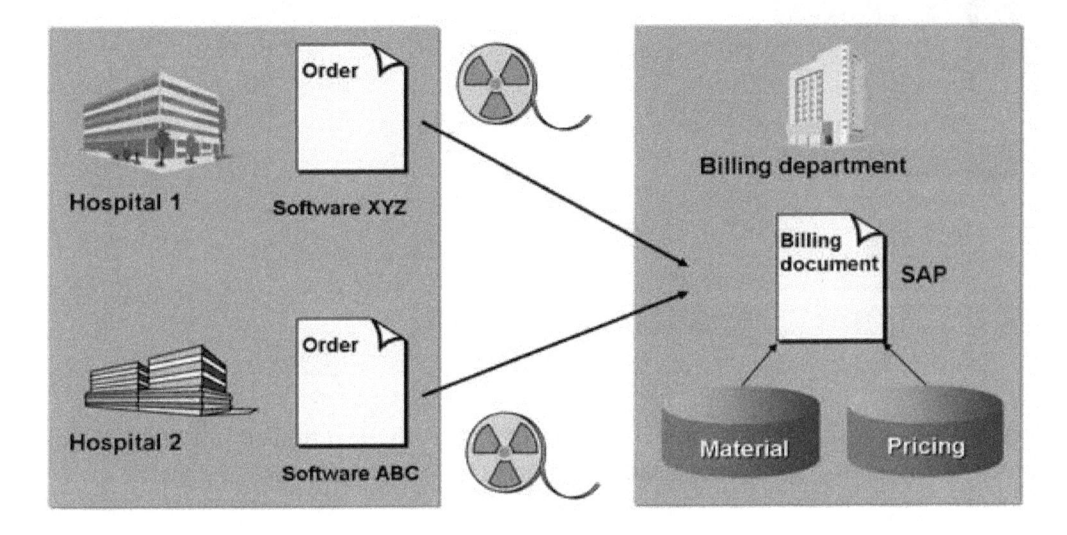

Using the general billing interface, you can invoice external documents in the SAP system (that is, orders and deliveries not created in the SAP system).

To do this, you must first:
- Prepare the data in a sequential file of specified format.
- Specify a minimum number of required fields to be filled from the data records.
- Specify the remaining fields required for billing either through the data records for the sequential file or through the system (optional fields).

Examples:

Required fields: Customer master, sales organization etc
Optional fields: Material master, price components etc

External reference numbers can be entered in the interface (such as external delivery numbers or external order numbers).

48. **Which of the following billing is often used for rental and service agreements?**
    (Only one answer is correct)

    (a) Periodic Billing
    (b) Milestone Billing
    (c) Ad-hoc Billing
    (d) None of the above

Answer: a

Explanation:

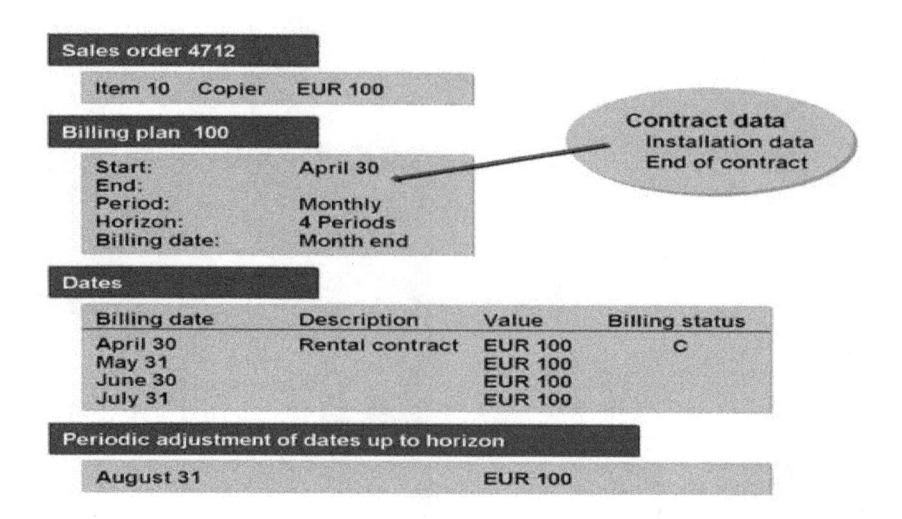

```
Sales order 4712
  Item 10   Copier    EUR 100
Billing plan  100
  Start:           April 30
  End:
  Period:          Monthly
  Horizon:         4 Periods
  Billing date:    Month end

Contract data
Installation data
End of contract

Dates
  Billing date   Description       Value      Billing status
  April 30       Rental contract   EUR 100    C
  May 31                           EUR 100
  June 30                          EUR 100
  July 31                          EUR 100

Periodic adjustment of dates up to horizon
  August 31                        EUR 100
```

Periodic billing can be used, for example, for transactions involving rental contracts. The contract data stored in the system can then be used as the basis for creating the billing plan.

The start and end dates define the duration of the billing plan. If possible, they are taken from the contract data. You may decide not to set an end date (if the durations unlimited). In this case, new dates can be extended to the horizon (the horizon specifies the number of settlement periods that are set in the billing plan).

New dates can be created either directly in the billing plan, or using the report RVFPLA01. You should schedule the report to run at regular intervals, since new dates are not compiled automatically when individual settlement periods are billed.

Billing dates can be used to determine when and how often billing is carried out, for example, on the first day or the last day of every month.

49. Which of the following are the examples of a Billing document type?
    (There are three correct answers to the question)

    (a) Pro-forma Invoice
    (b) Debit memo
    (c) Credit Memo
    (d) Intercompany delivery and Billing

Answer: a, b, c

Explanation:

Credit and Debit Memos
Credit and debit memos can be created either with reference to credit or debit memo requests (sales documents), or, if your company does not require a release procedure in the case of complaints, directly with reference to a billing document.

You can create credit and debit memo requests:

- Without reference to a previous business transaction
- With reference to an order
- With reference to a billing document

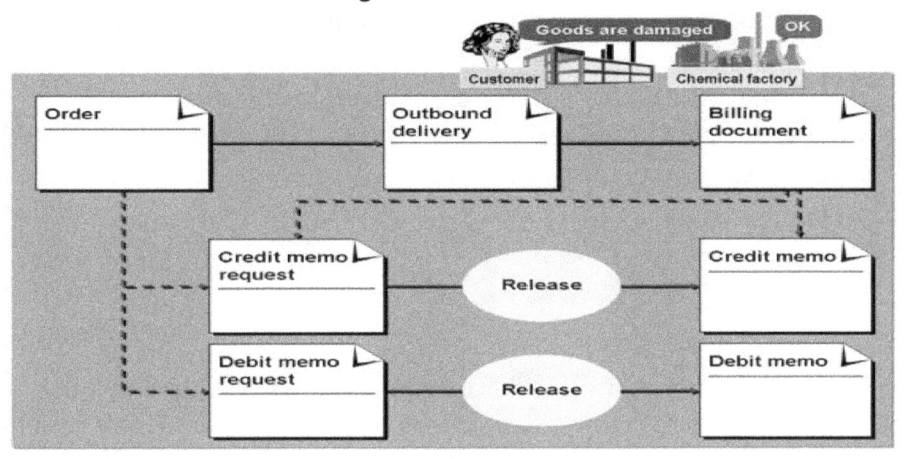

Pro forma Invoices

Pro forma invoices can be created for your foreign trade transactions. You also make over-the counter sales, which means that customers pay immediately and take the goods away with them.

Billing types for pro forma invoices are available for export transactions. You can create pro forma invoices with reference to orders or deliveries. You do not need to post the goods issue before creating a delivery-related pro forma invoice. You can create as many pro forma invoices as required, since the billing status in the reference document is not updated. Data from pro forma invoices is not transferred to Accounting.

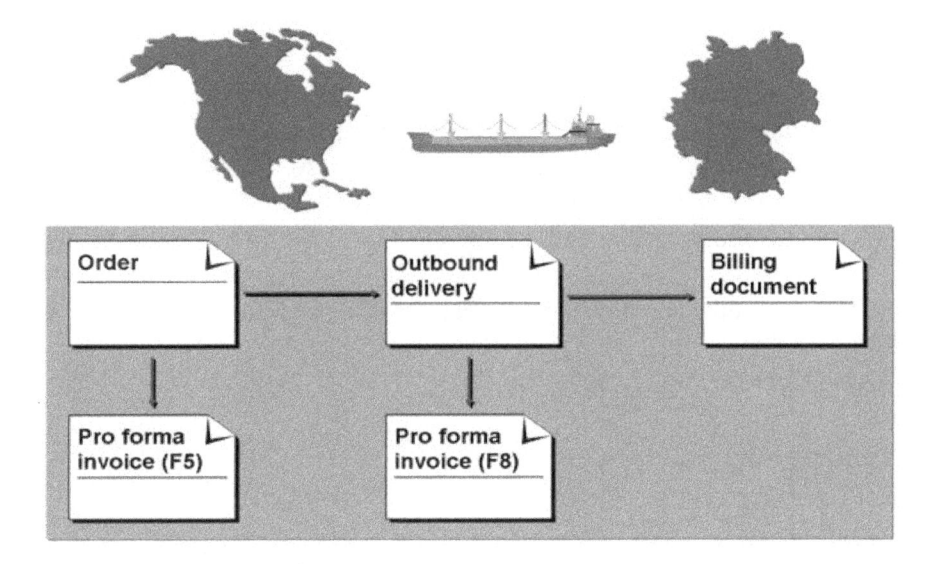

50. Which of the following statements are true regarding payment card processing?
    (There are two correct answers to the question)

(a) A payment card plan containing the card number, the card type and the authorization data is assigned to individual items in the sales order.
(b) When the delivery is created, a validity check is carried out for the authorization. If, for example, the authorization is no longer valid, then the authorization is automatically carried out again.
(c) The payment card data is copied to the billing document from the order.
(d) Both the payment card data and the authorization data are forwarded when the billing document is transferred to Accounting.

Answer: c, d

Explanation:

When you create a sales order, you can enter credit card data manually, or copy it from the payer master record. You can enter one card in the sales order overview screen. You are able to enter multiple cards or multiple authorizations on one card, in the payment card plan in the sales order header. The system automatically authorizes the sales order when you save it.

At a later time, you create the delivery. The authorization may have expired in the meantime, so the system checks to ensure that it is still valid. If the authorization is no longer valid, the system tells you to reinitiate authorization in the sales order. You complete and save the delivery.

When all the items are picked packed, and goods issue is posted, you create a billing document. Here, payment card data is copied from the sales order, or uploaded directly into the billing document from an external system, as in the case of point of sale. The system uses the authorizations in the payment card plan to calculate billing amounts. You process the billing document and release it to Financial Accounting.

When you release the billing document, the system copies the payment card information, billing amount, and authorization information into the accounting document. In accounting, receivables are posted to a special cash clearing account for the clearing house. The appropriate settlement process is then carried out according to the category of the card used. For instance, if a procurement card is used, additional data about the purchase is submitted for settlement.

51. Which of the following data can be changed once the billing document has been released to accounts?
    (Only one answer is correct)

    (a) Billing Date
    (b) Pricing
    (c) Output data
    (d) Account determination

Answer: c

Explanation:

The system sends billing data in invoices, credit memos and debit memos to Financial Accounting and posts them to the correct accounts. You can change the following data before an accounting document is created:

- Billing date
- Pricing
- Account determination
- Output determination data

After the billing document has been released to accounts. you can only change output data.

52. Which of the following number is used for clearing?
   (Only one answer is correct)

   (a) Reference number
   (b) Assignment number
   (c) Purchase order number
   (d) Delivery number

Answer: a

Explanation:

You can automatically fill the Reference and Assignment fields in the accounting document with numbers from the Sales and Distribution documents.

The reference number is in the header of the accounting document and is used for clearing. The assignment number is in the customer line item and is used for sorting line numbers. In

Customizing for copying control in billing, you can define the numbers that will be copied as reference or assignment numbers.

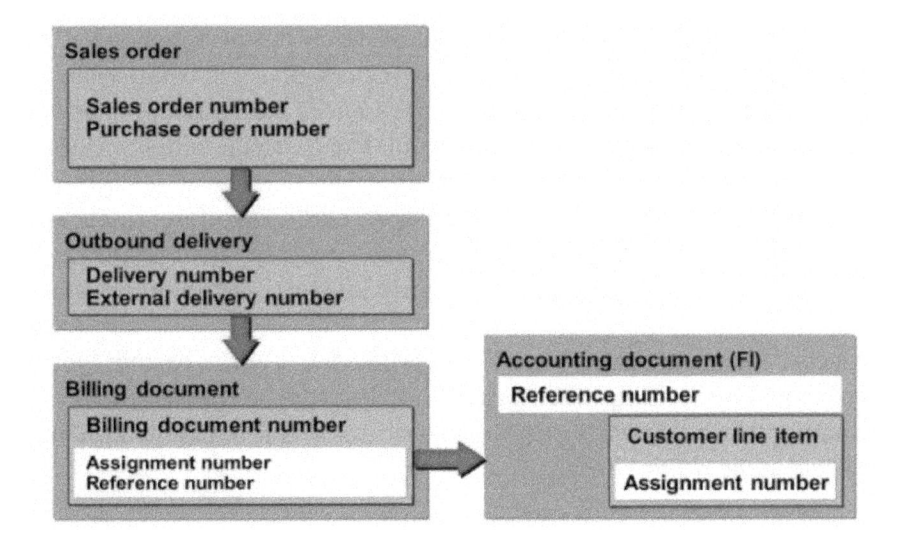

53. While maintaining the master data in which of the following ways you can represent the relationship between the head offices and its branches?
(There are two correct answers to the question)

(a) Partner functions
(b) Head office field
(c) Accounting field
(d) Relationship Field

Answer: a, b

Explanation:

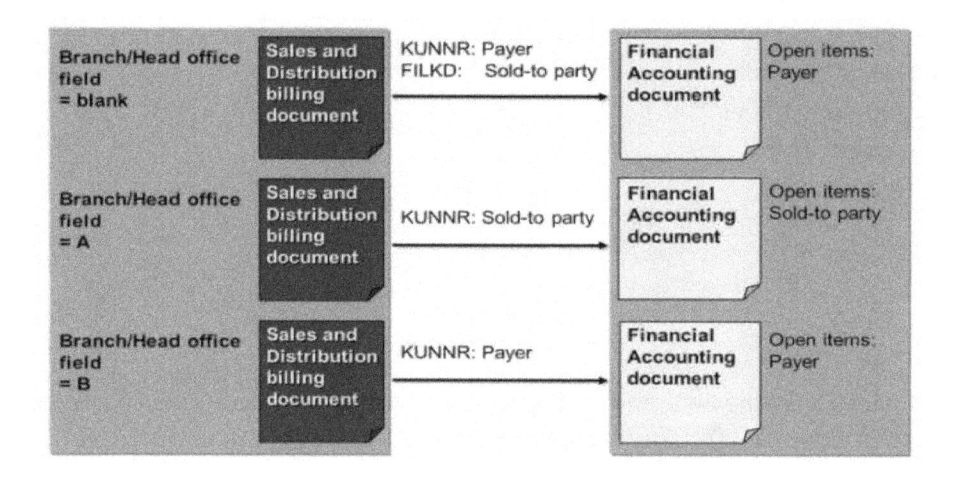

When maintaining master data, you can represent the relationship between the head office and its branches.

You can represent this relationship either with the partner functions in Sales and Distribution, or with the Head office field in the accounting segment of the customer master record.

Until now you had to maintain the accounting segment completely for this function for both customers. If accounting data was missing for the branch, the system could create billing documents for the branch, but could not transfer them to Financial Accounting. The partner functions in Sales and Distribution vary enormously according to customer requirements.

For example, the sold-to party can also function as the ship-to party. Therefore, customers asked whether it would be possible not to have to maintain the accounting segment if the branch of a company acted as the sold-to party and therefore, as a pure Sales and Distribution customer.

You can use the Branch/Head office field in the billing type to control which partner functions in the billing document should be transferred to Financial Accounting. The characteristics of this field then decide whether the sold-to party or the payer should be entered in the KUNNR (customer number) field in the billing header.

If you leave this field blank, the system will ignore any relationship stored in the Financial Accounting Head office field. For all the other settings. the relationship stored in Financial Accounting has priority over the relationship described by the sales and Distribution partner functions.

54. Which of the following rules are available that you want to use for determining the business area for each sales area?
    (Only one answer is correct)

    (a) Plant and item division
    (b) Sales Area
    (c) Item division
    (d) All of the above

Answer: d

Explanation:

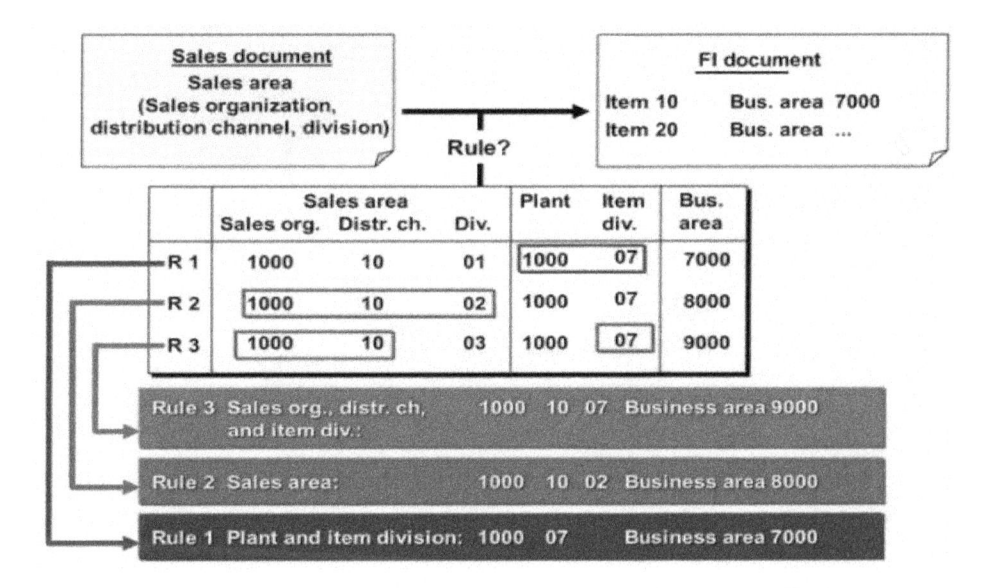

You can specify the rules you want to use for determining the business area for each sales area. The following rules are available (these rules cannot be extended):

- Business area assignment by plant and item division
- Business area assignment by sales area
- Business area assignment by sales organization, distribution channel, and item division

This can lead to different business areas being determined for several items within the same order. The system will automatically create several accounts receivable posting lines for the relevant business areas when this occurs.

Smart Business

55. In order fulfilment process, which of the following contains all the relevant information to process the customer request throughout the whole process cycle?
(Only one answer is correct)

   (a) Sales Order
   (b) Outbound delivery
   (c) Picking
   (d) Billing Document

Answer: a

Explanation:

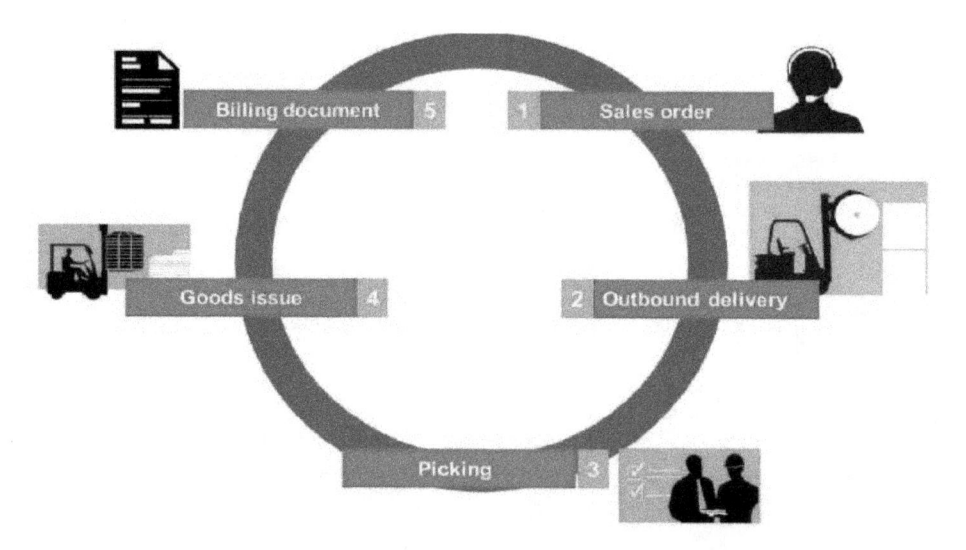

When a customer orders goods or services, a sales order is created to represent this process step. The sales order contains all the relevant information to process the customer request throughout the whole process cycle.
The system automatically copies data from master records and control tables that have been previously prepared.

56. Which of the following are created with reference to one or more sales order?
(There are two correct answers to the question)

   (a) Sales order
   (b) Outbound deliveries
   (c) Billing document
   (d) Payment Invoice

Answer: b, c

Explanation:

Outbound deliveries are normally created with reference to one or more sales orders. In that way, the relevant information (such as materials and quantities) can be copied from the sales order to the delivery.

The delivery document controls, supports, and monitors numerous process steps, such as:
- Picking
- Packing
- Transport planning and monitoring
- Posting the goods issue

After the distribution process has been completed, you can create the billing documents. This can be done with reference to one or more outbound deliveries when selling physical products) or with reference to sales orders when selling services). In both cases, the relevant information is copied from the preceding documents into the billing document.

57. A production order has which of the following functions?
(Only one answer is correct)

(a) Scheduling
(b) Costing
(c) Printing of Order papers
(d) All of the above

Answer: d

Explanation:

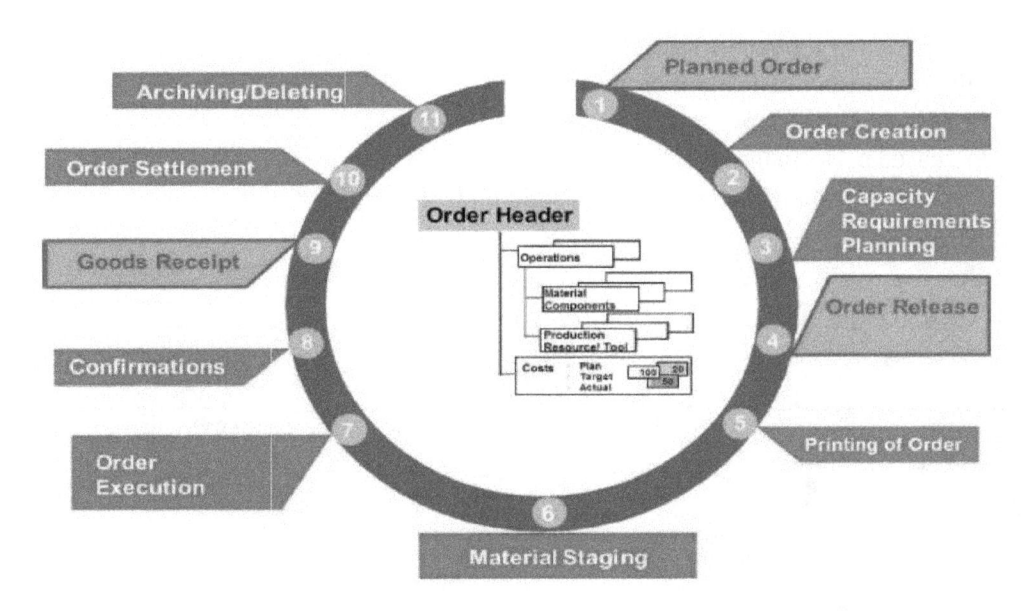

A production order has the following functions:
• Status management
• Scheduling

- Calculation of capacity requirements
- Costing
- Availability checks - material, PRT, and capacity
- Printing of order papers
- Material staging by using reservations
- Confirmation of quantities, activities, and time events (variable confirmation procedures)
- Goods receipt
- Period-end closing - process cost allocation, overhead rate, work in process (WIP) determination, variance calculation, and order settlement
- Archiving and retrieval

58. **Which of the following are the main simplifications of the S/4 HANA Sales data model? (There are two correct answers to the question)**

    (a) Elimination of Business data
    (b) Elimination of Index tables
    (c) Elimination of Status table
    (d) Elimination of contract data

Answer: b, c

Explanation:

Main simplifications of the data model are:
- Elimination of status tables
- Simplification of document flow
- Field length extensions
- Elimination of redundancies (for example, document index tables)

Key benefits of these simplifications are as follows:
- Reduced memory footprint
- Increased performance of SAP HANA queries
- Functional scope enhancements by extended field lengths

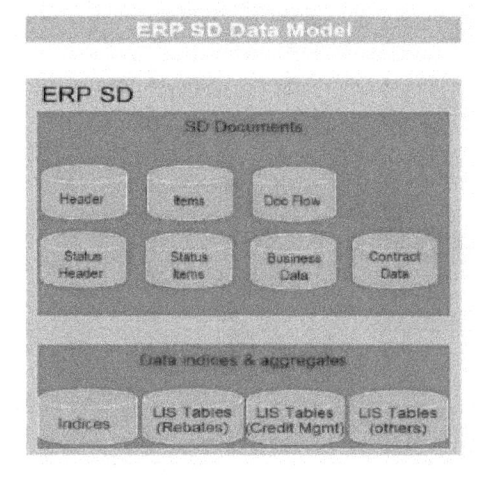

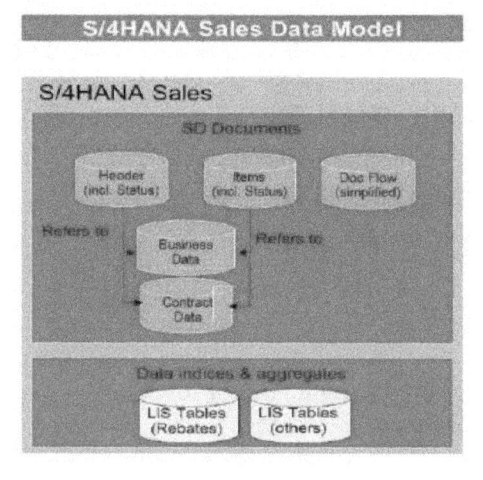

59. Business partners can be categorized as following?
    (There are three correct answers to the question)

    (a) Person
    (b) Organization
    (c) Group
    (d) Vendor

Answer: a, b, c

Explanation:

There are redundant object models in the traditional SAP ERP system where the vendor masters and customer master is used. The (mandatory) target approach in SAP S/4HANA is the Business Partner approach.

By using this approach, it is possible to manage master data for customers and vendors centrally. Business partners can be categorized as a person, group, or organization (legal person or part of a legal entity, for example, department).

An organization represents units such as a company, a department of a company, or an association. Organization is an umbrella term to map every kind of situation in the day-to-day business activities.

A group represents a shared living arrangement, a married couple, or an executive board.

60. In contrast to the traditional system, Sales order fulfilment app for S/4 HANA provides which of the following features?
    (There are two correct answers to the question)

    (a) Provides a prioritized list to Sales representative
    (b) Provides Collaboration features
    (c) Multiple reports need to be checked
    (d) Decision cannot be tracked in the system

Answer: a, b

Explanation:

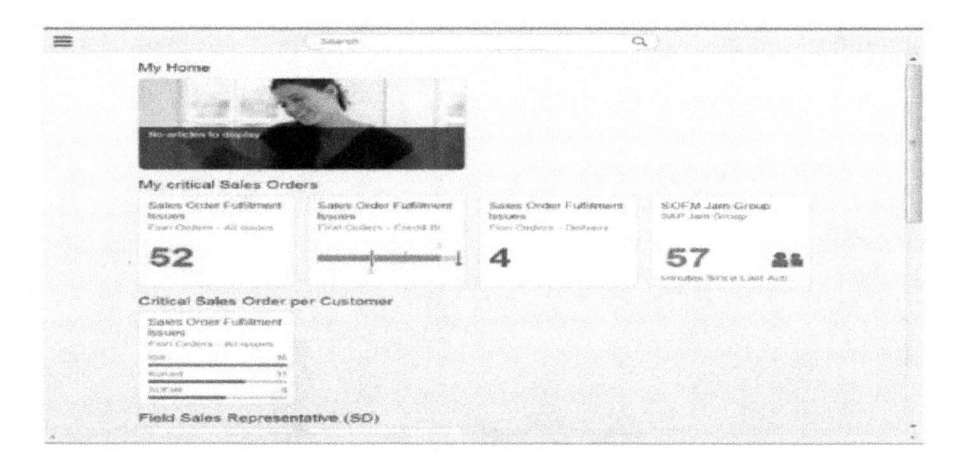

In contrast to the traditional system, SAP S/4HANA does the following:

- Provides the internal sales representative a big picture on the current sales order fulfillment situation so that he or she can decide which area to focus on with the follow-up activities.
- Offers the internal sales representative a prioritized list with the key characteristics of the sales order with unfinished overdue fulfillment process, in order to focus on the most important first.
- Supports the internal sales representative with the relevant insights, contacts and collaboration features.
- Enables the internal sales representative to run actions directly and document the solving progress via notes.

61. Which of the following are the features of SAP Smart Business Model?
    (There are two correct answers to the question)

    (a) New Working Model
    (b) User Experience
    (c) Delightful
    (d) Role Based Accessibility

Answer: a, b

Explanation:

SAP Smart Business is a general tool for the new user experience, combining modern working models with consumer-grade usability. This allows key roles to stay on top of their business. Making better and faster decisions by letting end users touch, analyze, share and act in real-time.

Real-time insights are combined with analytics and transactional follow-up activities to allow better and faster decisions and the new consumer-grade, responsive and consistent user interface supports multiple channels.

> SAP Smart Business is a general tool for the new User Experience, combining modern working models with a consumer-grade usability. This allows key roles to stay on top of their business making better and faster decisions by letting end users touch, analyze, share and act in real-time.

Combining **real-time insights** with analytics and transactional **follow-up activities** to allow **better and faster decisions**

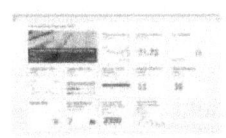

New working model

New **consumer-grade, responsive** and consistent user interface supporting **multiple channels**

User Experience

62. Which of the following scenario delivered by SAP allows you to resolve the sales order from being fulfilled?
(Only one answer is correct)

(a) SAP Smart Business for Cash Management
(b) SAP Smart Business for Project Execution
(c) SAP Smart Business for purchasing
(d) SAP Smart Business for Sales Order Fulfilment

Answer: d

Explanation:

The SAP Smart Business modeler apps are a set of SAP Fiori apps that you use to create and manage SAP Smart Business entities.

Smart Business entities allow your company to define, manage, and leverage consistent KPIs across all your business apps (for example reporting tools, dashboards and custom-built apps).

The SAP Smart Business modeler apps are as follows:

- Create KPI
- Create Evaluation
- Manage KPI Authorizations
- Configure KPI Tiles
- Configure KPI Drill-Down
- Manage KPI Associations
- KPI Workspace
- Migration Tool

There are predefined scenarios delivered by SAP like:

- SAP Smart Business for Cash Management
- SAP Smart Business for Project Execution
- SAP Smart Business for My Quotation Pipeline
- SAP Smart Business for Purchasing
- SAP Smart Business for Sales Order Fulfillment

SAP Smart Business for sales order fulfillment is an SAP Smart Business cockpit that allows you to resolve issues that impede sales orders from being fulfilled. The cockpit offers you a list of all sales orders that cannot be completed for one or more reasons.

The cockpit highlights impediments, and provides supporting information and specific options to resolve issues. This allows you to monitor sales orders in critical stages, collaborate with internal and external contacts, and efficiently address issues to ensure that sales orders in critical stages are fulfilled as fast as possible.

63. **If certain items in the BOM are to be made relevant to sales documents, which of the following help in achieving the same?**
    (Only one answer is correct)

    (a) Mark the items as relevant to Sales manually.
    (b) Sales and Distribution is used to create the BOM, in that case items are automatically marked as relevant for sales
    (c) Usage indicator 5 is used to create the BOM; in that case items are automatically marked as relevant for sales
    (d) The items in the BOM cannot be made relevant for sales

Answer: c

Explanation:

The item has been set to the status "relevant to sales".
When you create a BOM, this status is automatically activated because the BOM has been created as a Sales and Distribution BOM.

The bill of material (BOM) contains the assemblies or components that are involved in the production of a material. BOMs are used in the following applications:

- Material requirements planning
- Production
- Procurement
- Product costing

64. An order is placed for your products, and you want purchase requisition creation to take place automatically for the components of these products. Where will it be accomplished?
(Only one answer is correct)

   (a) Item Category at Purchase Requisition
   (b) Item Category at Sales Order
   (c) Customizing of Purchase requisition
   (d) Schedule Lines at Sales Order

Answer: d

Explanation:

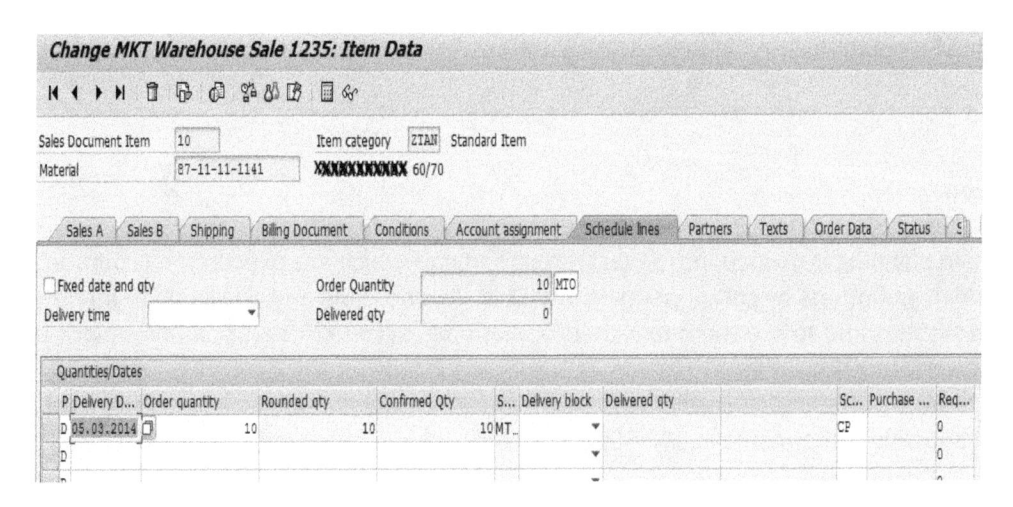

All the necessary information is contained in the schedule lines in the sales order. Important control parameters were already determined for purchase requisition creation when you defined the schedule line category in the sales order.

65. Which of the following is the correct statement that describes the role of delivery document for shipping processing?
(There are three correct answers to the question)

   (a) It forms the basis for all various activities from packing to issuing of goods
   (b) It is used in various business transactions
   (c) The status settings in the delivery document provide information on the progress of different steps within shipping processing.
   (d) It is a mandatory step for billing document

Answer: a, b, c

Explanation:

- It forms the basis for all various activities, such as Packing, Printing and distributing shipping documents, processing the goods issue etc.
- It is used in various business transactions; the status settings in the delivery document provide information on the progress of different steps within shipping processing.
- It is a NOT a mandatory step for Billing document

66. **Which of the following components in SAP SCM helps in supply chain planning?**
    (Only one answer is correct)

    (a) Demand Planning
    (b) ATP Check
    (c) SNP
    (d) All of the above

Answer: d

Explanation:

Supply chain planning is divided into several steps some of which are executed by components in SAP S/4HANA and others by components in SAP SCM. It is possible and advisable to integrate these two systems and to use them together for planning. System integration takes place using the Core Interface (CIF).

Use the respective components in SAP SCM to accomplish the following processes:

- Demand Planning (DP)
- Global Available-to-Promise check (ATP check)
- Supply Network Planning (SNP)
- Production Planning and Detailed Scheduling (PP/DS)

DP forecasts future customer requirements using past sales figures and other inputs to generate Planned Independent Requirements. They can be consumed using requirements strategies in SAP S/4 HANA.

67. **Which of the following is built on SAP HANA, cloud deployment to deliver integrated unified planning?**
    (Only one answer is correct)

    (a) Supply Network planning
    (b) Demand Planning
    (c) Integrated Business Planning
    (d) All of the above

Answer: d

Explanation:

Integrated Business Planning (IBP)

Supply Chain Monitoring
Supply Chain Control Tower

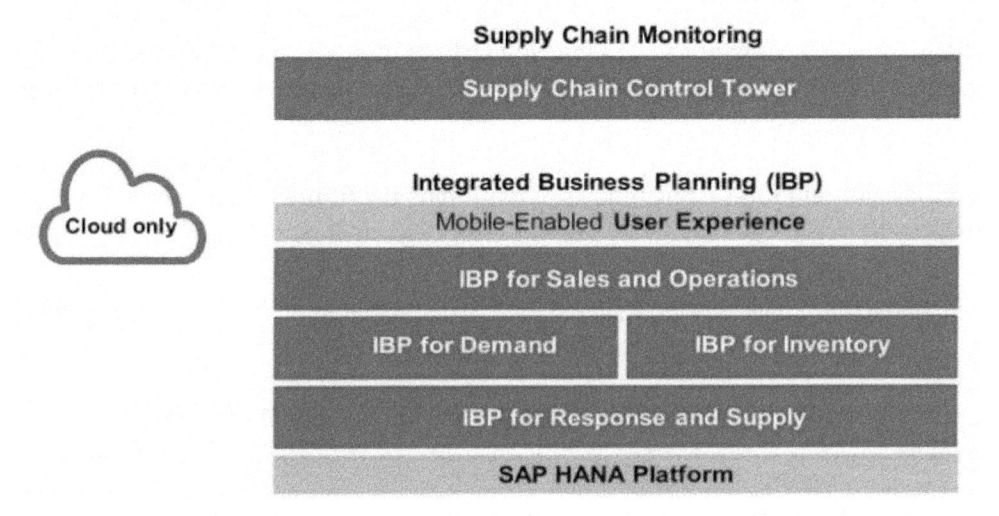

Cloud only

Integrated Business Planning (IBP)
Mobile-Enabled User Experience
IBP for Sales and Operations
IBP for Demand — IBP for Inventory
IBP for Response and Supply
SAP HANA Platform

SAP Integrated Business Planning (IBP) is a new, state-of-the art platform for real-time, integrated supply chain planning. It is built on SAP HANA, for Cloud deployment. SAP IBP is being developed to deliver integrated unified planning, across sales and operations, demand, Inventory, supply and response planning as well as the supply chain control tower for dashboard analytics and monitoring.

SAP IBP delivers a new paradigm of user experience and efficiency, leveraging real-time dashboards advanced predictive analytics. interactive simulation, embedded social collaboration and Microsoft Excel-enabled planning tables.

68. Which of the following is a list of standard forecasting techniques?
   (Only one answer is correct)

   (a) Moving Average
   (b) Constant Model
   (c) Exponential smoothing
   (d) All of the above

Answer: d

Explanation:

Historical data can forecast future market demand. Mathematical techniques are used for this purpose.

The following is a list of Standard forecasting techniques:

- Moving average

- Constant model
- Trend model
- Seasonal model
- Exponential smoothing

You can choose the type of historical data that you want to forecast. You can use any key figure. You can forecast material consumptions, incoming order quantities, invoiced quantities, or sales revenues.

The system uses different forecasting models to determine the future pattern of the key figure in question.

You can use various constant models for products with historical data that changes little over time.

You can use seasonal models for seasonal products, such as ice cream, Easter candies, or Christmas lights.

There are options for smoothing and time-dependent weighting of historical data, as well as outlier corrections.

69. Bill of Materials are used in which of the following applications?
(There are three correct answers to the question)

(a) Production
(b) Procurement
(c) Product Costing
(d) Manufacturing

Answer: a, b, c

Explanation:

The Bill of Material (BOM) contains the assemblies or components that are involved in the production of a material. BOMs are used in the following applications:
- Material Requirements Planning
- Production
- Procurement
- Product costing

Basic Functions (customizing)

70. **Sales documents can be customized at which of the following levels?**
    (Only one answer is correct)

    (a) Header
    (b) Item
    (c) Schedule Line
    (d) All of the above

Answer: d

Explanation:

Sales processes are controlled by Customizing for sales documents. Customizing for sales documents can be done at the header, item or schedule line levels depending on the structure of the document. Sales documents can be controlled through the sales document type, item category, and schedule line category.

You must make settings in Customizing so that the item and schedule line categories are determined automatically in the sales document.

To completely set up a business process in your system you need to configure the system to forward the necessary data from the sales document to subsequent documents. You can do this by using copying control.

71. **Which of the following are the basic sales functions?**
    (There are two correct answers to the question)

    (a) Pricing
    (b) Material Determination
    (c) Material Master
    (d) Billing

Answer: a, b

Explanation:

Some of the basic sales functions are as follows:

- Partner determination
- Pricing
- Output determination
- Text determination
- Material determination
- Credit management

- Incompleteness
- Delivery scheduling

You can finalize the minute details of these basic functions at each level within the sales document. The sales document is not completely configured until you process all the necessary basic functions.

For example, for pricing, you can set up your pricing procedure for a sales document type. First you must configure the sales document type and pricing procedure separately, and then assign the procedure to the sales document type.

You can also create default output types for each sales document type. To do this assign the relevant output determination procedure to the sales document type in Customizing for the output.

You can use different functions for different sales document types. For example, pricing updates are needed to create an inquiry: inventory updates are not needed to create an inquiry.

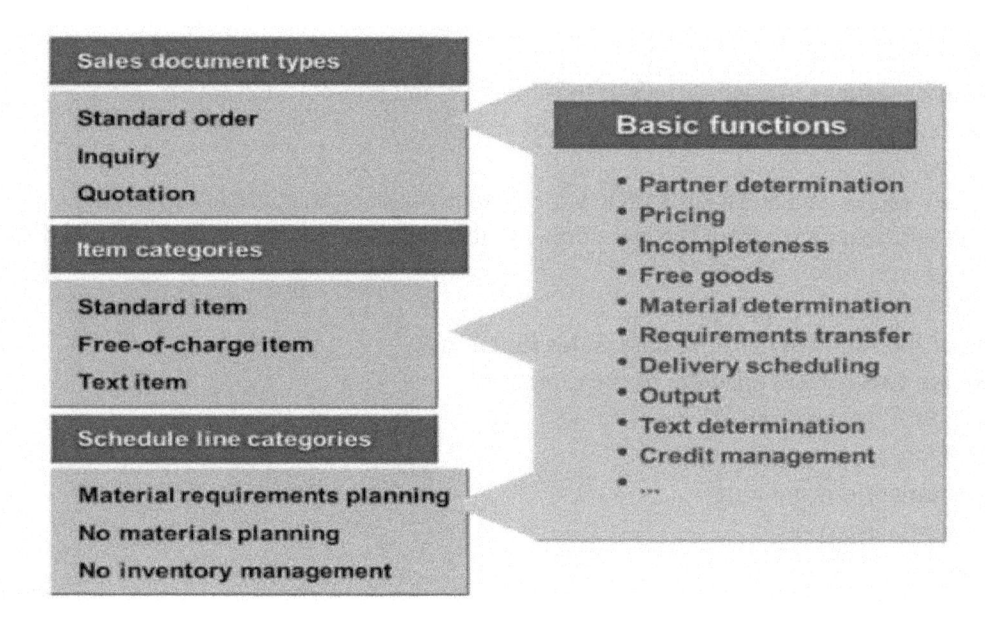

Sales document types
- Standard order
- Inquiry
- Quotation

Item categories
- Standard item
- Free-of-charge item
- Text item

Schedule line categories
- Material requirements planning
- No materials planning
- No inventory management

Basic functions
- Partner determination
- Pricing
- Incompleteness
- Free goods
- Material determination
- Requirements transfer
- Delivery scheduling
- Output
- Text determination
- Credit management
- ...

72. Which of the following settings are customized for the sales document type that influences the sales process?
    (There are two correct answers to the question)

    (a) Sales document Category
    (b) Schedule Line Item Categories
    (c) Item Category
    (d) Delivery and billing blocks

Answer: a, d

Explanation:

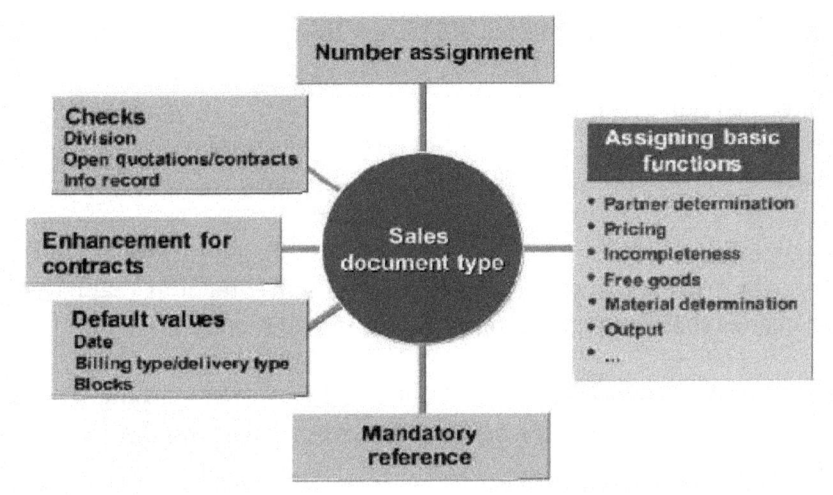

[Diagram: Sales document type with connections to:
- Number assignment
- Checks (Division, Open quotations/contracts, Info record)
- Enhancement for contracts
- Default values (Date, Billing type/delivery type, Blocks)
- Mandatory reference
- Assigning basic functions (Partner determination, Pricing, Incompleteness, Free goods, Material determination, Output, ...)]

In Customizing for the sales document type, you configure the settings that influence the sales process.
Some of these settings are as follows:
- Sales document category
- Delivery and billing blocks
- Document types for deliveries and billing documents

You can also define some default values for the document creation. You can overwrite these values at various levels of the document to match particular procedures such as the delivery date requested by the customer or certain basic requirements for contracts.

In addition, you can activate various checks such as messages about open quotations or outline agreements searches for customer-specific material information records or checks for the credit limit. Note that activating checks can affect the system performance.

73. Which of the following settings allows you to decide based on the essential characteristics of Item category?
    (There are two correct answers to the question)

    (a) Pricing
    (b) Billable item
    (c) Categorical Item
    (d) Line Items

Answer: a, b

Explanation:

The Item category controls the way an item functions in the sales document and in any subsequent processing for the business transaction.

The essential characteristics of an item category enable you to decide on the following settings:

- Whether the business data in the item can be different from that of the document header
- Whether pricing applies to the item
- Whether and how the item is billed
- Whether the item refers to a material or whether it is just a text item
- Which incompleteness procedure is used to check the item data

You can change the item category settings that are defined in the standard system. You can also define new item categories. You must always copy the existing item categories that have already been tested and then change these categories to meet your requirements.

The delivery relevance indicator is only for items without schedule lines. For example, you can indicate that a text item is relevant to delivery, so that the system copies this item from the sales order into the delivery document.

74. **Which of the following Item category function is relevant for billing?**
    (Only one answer is correct)

    (a) Text Item for Inquiry
    (b) Standard Item for quotation
    (c) Standard Item for Order
    (d) Free-of-charge item for order

Answer: c

Explanation:

The figure shows examples of item categories, with the relevant settings that are provided in the SAP standard system. Every item in a sales document is controlled by its item category.

As a result, you can use more than one item category in a sales document type. This enables you to realize a specific business process for each item in the sales document.

	Function	Example
Text item for inquiry	No pricing Schedule lines permitted Not relevant for billing	AFTX
Standard item for quotation	Pricing Schedule lines permitted Not relevant for billing	AGN
Standard item for order	Pricing Schedule lines permitted Relevant for billing	TAN
Free-of-charge item for order	No pricing Schedule lines permitted Not relevant for billing	TANN

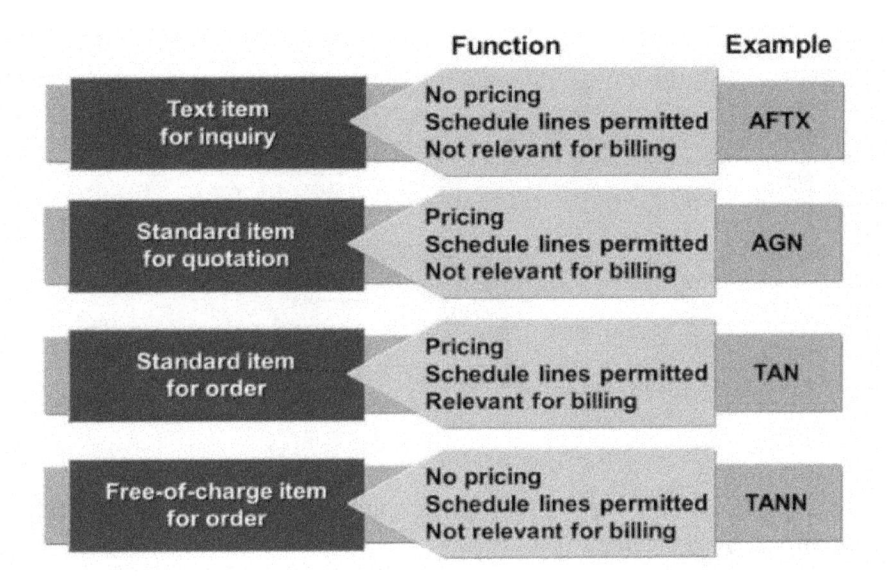

You can configure the functions of the item categories according to your requirements.

Examples of such configurations are as follows:

- You do not need price determination for the text item in the inquiry (the item category AFTX), but you want to enter delivery quantities and delivery dates. Therefore, you allow schedule lines.
- You want schedule lines for a free-of-charge item in the sales order (the item category TANN), but you do not want to carry out pricing for this item or transfer it to billing.

75. **Suppose a customer orders 100 units of material M1 and the customer receives 10 units of material M2 free of charge. Which of the following is the correct way of defining this condition in Sales Item category?**
    (Only one answer is correct)

    (a) Enter the item 10 in lower level item field for the item 20
    (b) Enter the item 20 in higher level item field for the item 10
    (c) Enter the item 10 in higher level item field for the item 20
    (d) This condition is not possible to define in the standard SAP system

Answer: c

Explanation:

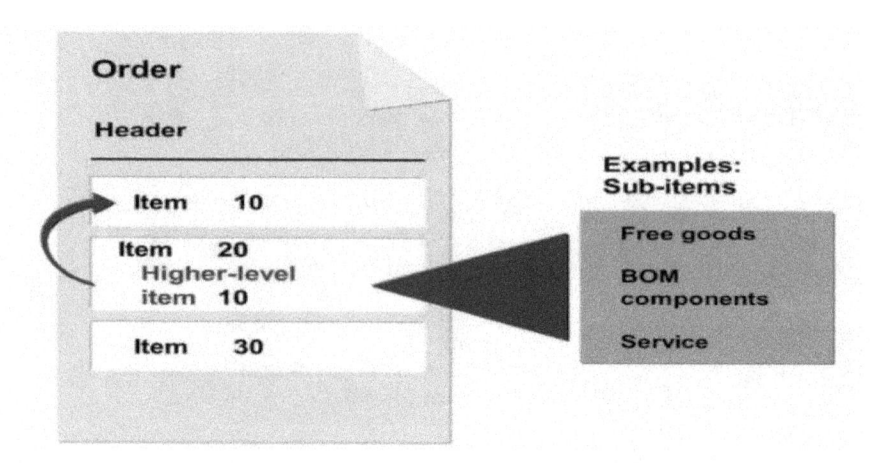

You can assign an item to a higher-level item if for example; a customer receives free goods for ordering a certain quantity of your product.

The following table illustrates this scenario:

Item	Material	Quantity	Price
Item 10	M1	100 units	Euro 1000
Item 20	M2	10 units	free of charge

If the customer orders 100 units of material Ml, the customer receives 10 units of material M2 free of charge. To display this condition, you enter the item 10 in the higher-level item field for the item 20.

This simple form of supplying free goods is supplemented with automatic determination of free goods. Other examples for using sub-items include the explosion of bills of material (BOMB) or service items in sales documents.

Hint: Alternative items can also be recorded in quotations and inquiries in addition to sub-items Alternative items are treated different from sub-items. For example, alternative items are not included in the net value of the document.

76. Which of the following Schedule Lines in Sales documents are not relevant for delivery? (Only one answer is correct)

   (a) Schedule line in quotation
   (b) Material Requirement planning in order
   (c) Schedule line in returns
   (d) Schedule line in item category

Answer: a

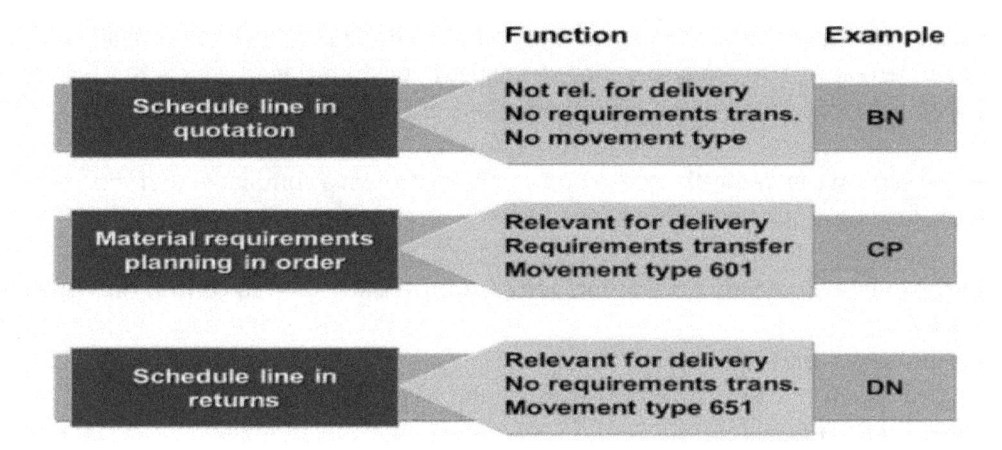

Explanation:

	Function	Example
Schedule line in quotation	Not rel. for delivery / No requirements trans. / No movement type	BN
Material requirements planning in order	Relevant for delivery / Requirements transfer / Movement type 601	CP
Schedule line in returns	Relevant for delivery / No requirements trans. / Movement type 651	DN

Schedule lines in quotations are not relevant for delivery. The requirement transfer is inactive in the schedule line category. Goods movements are not necessary in your warehouses. Therefore, no movement type is required.

Schedule lines from category CP are relevant for delivery. The requirement transfer is active in the schedule line category. Complete Customizing for requirement transfer, such as for requirements planning, requires you to define and assign a requirements class the goods movement is controlled by the movement type 601. With this movement type, when the goods issue for the delivery is posted, the system takes the quantity from the unrestricted use stocks.

If you want a returns delivery to follow a return order, you need a schedule line category that is relevant for delivery. In this case, requirement transfer is not necessary.

The movement type 651 ensures that a goods receipt goes to the blocked returns stock. This activity replaces the usual goods issue.

77. **Which of the following can be adjusted in the customizing of the sales document type? (There are two correct answers to the question)**

    (a) Billing relevance
    (b) Immediate Delivery
    (c) Scheduled delivery
    (d) Increment of Item number

Answer: b, d

Explanation:

The immediate delivery flag and the item number increment setting are made at document type level. Billing relevance is set at item category.

Customizing

The system uses the default values that you defined in Customizing for creating documents. For example, you can set a default value for the delivery date or configure a delivery or billing block in the sales document type. You can also define strategies in Customizing to enable the system to determine document information based on combinations of several criteria.

For example, the system can determine the shipping point through a combination of the delivering plant, loading group and shipping condition.

78. Which of the following control parameters are created at each level to control the copying procedure?
(Only one answer is correct)

(a) Routines for Data Transfer
(b) Copying requirements
(c) Switches
(d) All of the above

Answer: d

Explanation:

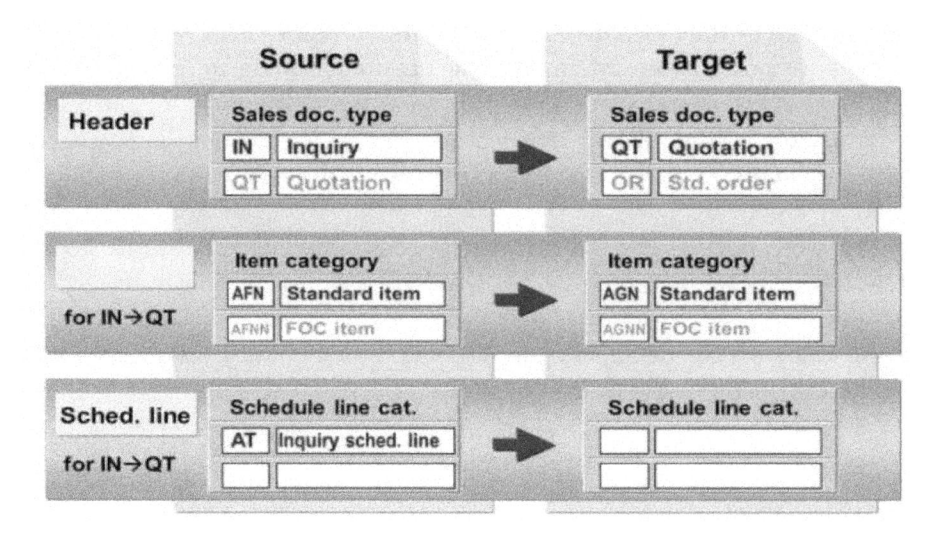

You set up copying controls for the header, item, and schedule line levels to match the structure of your sales document. To control the copying procedure, you create the following control parameters at each level:

Routines for data transfer
These routines control the transfer of fields from the source document to the target document.
Copying requirements

You define requirements that are checked when you create a document with reference. If these requirements are not met in a particular case, the system issues a warning or an error message and if required, terminates the processing.

Switches

There are switches for setting specific controls for each transaction. For example, you can activate or deactivate the transfer of item numbers from the preceding document at the header level for sales documents.

If you enter an invalid value or do not enter a target value at the item and schedule line levels, the system takes the target value from the assignment of the item or schedule line categories. Any value that you enter at the item and schedule line levels must exist as an alternative in the item or schedule line category assignment.

79. Which of the following copying requirement checks whether the item that is to be used as a copy has a reason for rejection or a completed status?
   (Only one answer is correct)

   (a) Copying requirement 001
   (b) Copying requirement 301
   (c) Copying requirement 501
   (d) None of the above

Answer: b
Explanation:

You can store copying requirements at every level in copying control. Copying requirements contain the specific requirements for each business process. The reference document can be created only if all these requirements have been met.

Examples of copying requirements that are included in the SAP standard system are as follows:

Header level
The copying requirement 001 checks, for instance, whether the sold-to party and sales area in the source and target documents are the same.
Item level
The copying requirement 301 checks, for instance, whether the item that is to be used as a copy has a reason for rejection or a completed status.
Schedule line level
The copying requirement 501 ensures that only schedule lines with an open quantity greater than zero are copied.

Note: Routines and requirements are written in the ABAP code, and they can be processed in Customizing for Sales and Distribution under System Modifications. In this Customizing option, check whether the existing objects are suitable. Normally, you can adjust your system quickly by copying the objects in the standard system and deleting or adding lines of code.

80. Which of the following status the item will be given when the customer rejects the item from the quotation because the product is too expensive?
(Only one answer is correct)

(a) In process
(b) Open
(c) Completed
(d) Partially referred

Answer: c

Explanation:

A customer rejection (using the reason for Rejection field) will set the item status to completed.
An in process status means that the item has not yet been fully completed.
An open status means that the document does not yet having any subsequent process created for it.
A partially referenced status mean that total order quantity has not yet been fully referenced in target sales document.

81. Which of the following can be used to activate or deactivate the transfer of item numbers from the preceding document at the header level for sales documents?
(Only one answer is correct)

(a) Routines
(b) Switches
(c) Copying Requirements
(d) All of the above

Answer: b

Explanation:

Switches are settings in Customizing. In this case, there is a switch that can be set to re-number items as they are referenced from a source document to a target document.
Routines are used to control the transfer of data from a source to a target document.
Copying requirements are standard or customer-defined rules that are checked during the copying process and, if the rules are not met. the process may halt.

Pricing and condition technique

82. **Which of the following criteria influence pricing procedure determination during pricing?**
    (There are three correct answers to the question)

    (a) Sales Area
    (b) Pricing procedure code in Customer master
    (c) Pricing procedure code in Company code
    (d) Pricing Procedure code in Document type

Answer: a, b, d

Explanation:

The determination of the procedure depends on the following factors:

- **Customer determination procedure:** You specify the customer determination procedure in the customer master record for each sales area.
- **Document pricing procedure:** You specify the document pricing procedure for each sales document type and billing type.

To determine the procedure, you allocate the customer determination procedure and the document pricing procedure to a pricing procedure within a sales area.

83. **Which of the following statements are incorrect regarding access sequence?**
    (There are two correct answers to the question)

    (a) An access sequence defines the sequence in which condition records for a condition type are found and read
    (b) Each access performed during the access sequence is made using a condition table
    (c) An access sequence consists of only one condition table
    (d) An access sequence is assigned to a condition type

Answer: c, d

Explanation:

- An access sequence is a search strategy that the system uses to find valid data for a particular condition type. It determines the sequence in which the system searches for data.
- The access sequence consists of one or more accesses. The sequence of the accesses establishes which condition records have priority over others.
- The accesses tell the system where to look first, second, and so on, until it finds a valid condition record. You specify an access sequence for each condition type for which you create condition records.

Condition type

- PR00 — Price — Access sequence PR02
- K007 — Discount % — Access sequence K007
- K020 — Major customer disc. — Access sequence K020

Access sequence — **Condition tables**

PR02
1. Customer / material
2. Price list / currency / material
3. Material

Specific → General

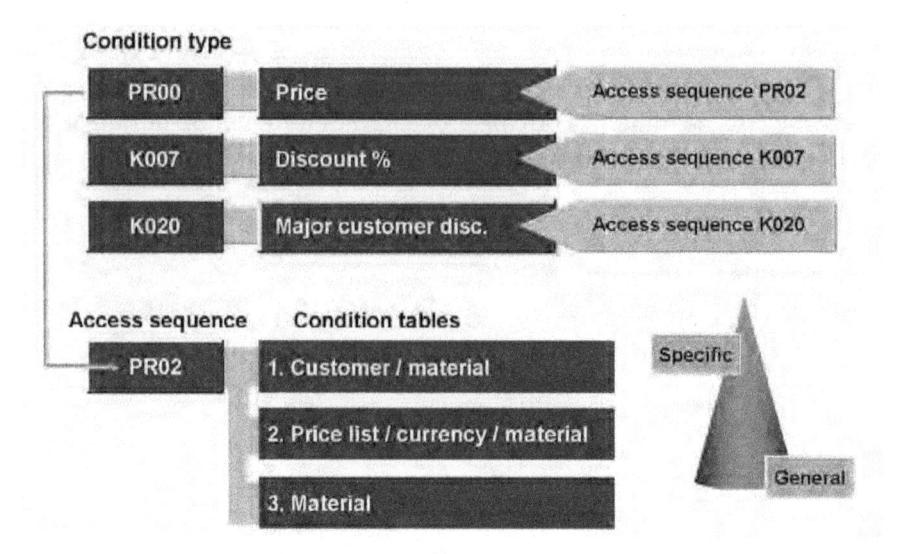

84. Which of the following statement is true regarding pricing types and re-pricing?
(There are two correct answers to the question)

(a) Copy control makes it possible to handle re-pricing of billing documents
(b) Re-pricing cannot be carried out in the billing document
(c) Pricing behavior can be configured in the Pricing Type
(d) Document types cannot be set to automatically do re-pricing when they are created

Answer: a, c

Explanation:

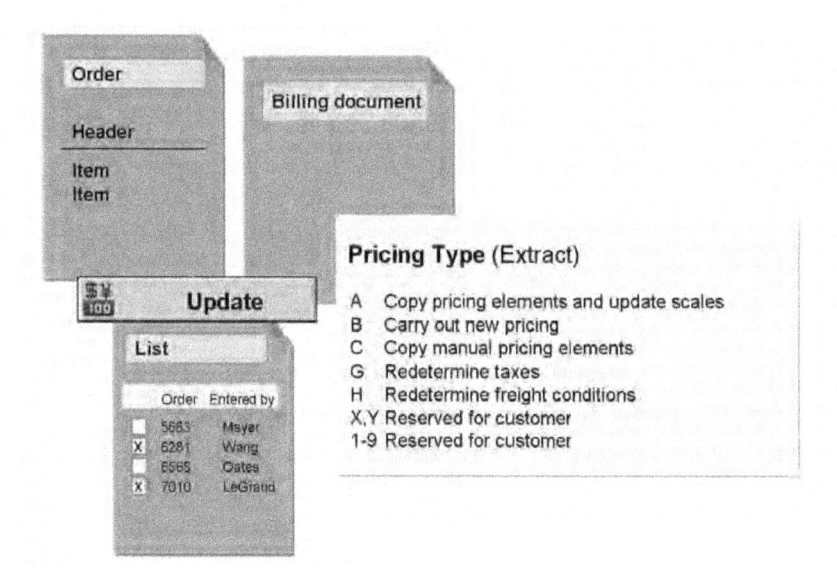

Pricing Type (Extract)

- A Copy pricing elements and update scales
- B Carry out new pricing
- C Copy manual pricing elements
- G Redetermine taxes
- H Redetermine freight conditions
- X,Y Reserved for customer
- 1-9 Reserved for customer

Pricing behavior can be configured in the Pricing type.
There are two options to control the new pricing function in the sales document:

- Update prices on the condition screens is available at the header and item levels. You can choose the pricing type in the dialog box that appears.
- To use the new pricing document function for the sales document (→ *Edit* → *New Pricing Document*); assign a pricing type to the pricing procedure in Customizing. If you do not maintain an entry, the system uses pricing type B (Carry out new pricing).

These functions are supported for both the sales and billing documents.

Copying control makes it possible to handle re-pricing of billing documents based on several different scenarios. While all customers will not use every pricing type, the ability to specify what will happen to pricing calculations during billing is a decision each customer must make.

85. **Which of the following statements are correct?**
    (There are two correct answers to the question)

    (a) Header condition HM00 allow you to enter the order value manually, and this price will be distributed proportionally across the items based on previous net value
    (b) Item Condition PN00 allows you to enter a net price per Item. This will deactivate any other pricing for that item.
    (c) PMIN is header condition that will check that you do not deal below a set minimum price. Whenever the net price is below the PMIN price the system will automatically adjust price to PMIN
    (d) Customer hierarchies consist of nodes without any validity periods

Answer: a, b
Explanation:

Header condition HM00 allow you to enter the order value manually, and this price will be distributed proportionally across the items based on previous net value Item Condition PN00 allows you to enter a net price per Item.

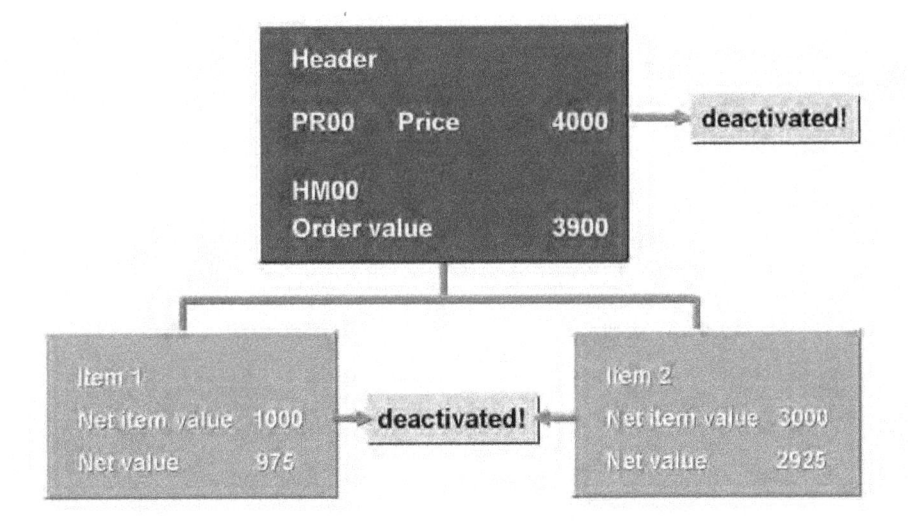

This will deactivate any other pricing for that item. Moreover, Rounding can be down up or down depending on the setting. Condition DIFF is group condition and is distributed across all items according to value.

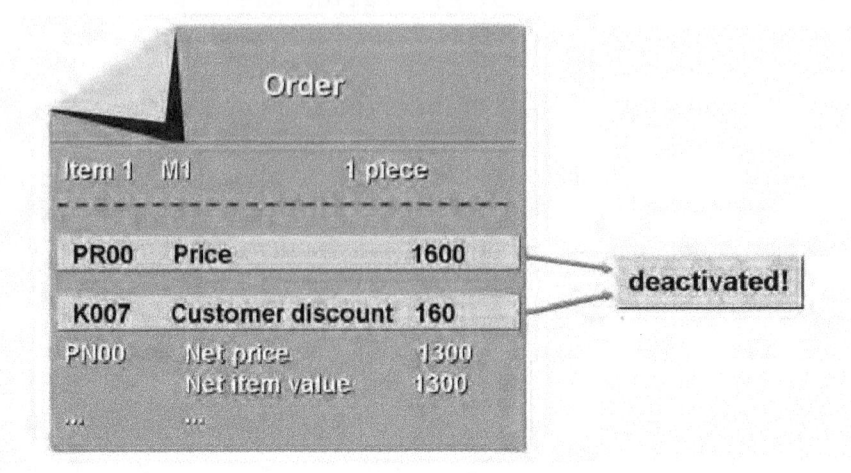

86. **Which of the following condition type is used to retrieve the standard cost of the material? (Only one answer is correct)**

    (a) VPRS
    (b) EDI1
    (c) MWST
    (d) SKTO

Answer: a

Explanation:

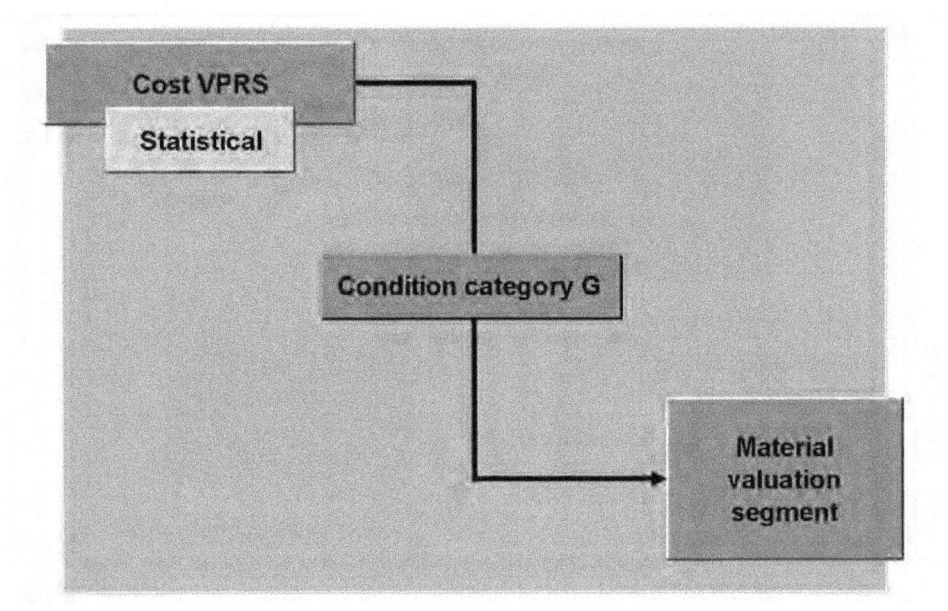

In the standard version, condition type VPRS is used to retrieve the standard cost of the material. The pricing procedure uses this condition type as a statistical value.

Using condition category G, VPRS accesses the valuation segment of the material master locating either the standard cost or the moving average cost, as specified in the material master.

Condition category S always accesses the standard cost, whereas condition category T always accesses the moving average cost.

The profit margin is calculated using formula 11 in the pricing procedure. This formula subtracts the cost from the net value.

87. **Which of the following must be activated for rebate processing?**
    (There are two correct answers to the question)

    (a) Sales Organization
    (b) Sold to party
    (c) Payer
    (d) Sales document type

Answer: a, c

Explanation:

To function properly, rebate processing must be activated for:
- The sales organization
- The payer master
- The billing document type

To improve performance, you should deactivate rebate processing if it is not necessary.

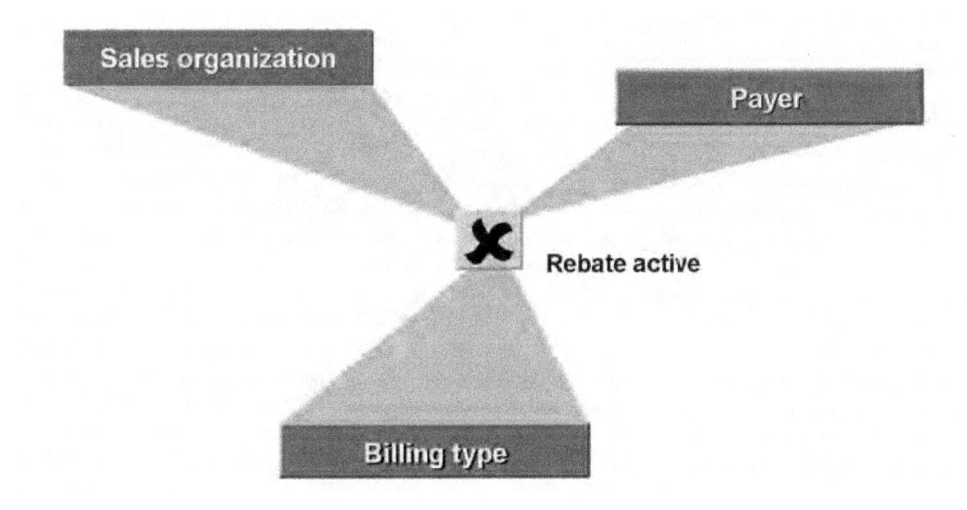

88. **Which of the following condition types is a group condition and is divided among all the items in an order according to value?**
(Only one answer is correct)

(a) PNOO
(b) AMIW
(c) PMIN
(d) AMIZ

Answer: b

Explanation:

You may create a minimum value for each order using condition type AMIW. If the value in the order header is less than this minimum order value during pricing, the system uses the minimum as the net order value automatically. The minimum order value is a statistical condition.

Condition type AMIW is a group condition and is divided among the different items according to value.

Calculation formula 13 is assigned to condition type AMIZ in the pricing procedure. This formula calculates the minimum value surcharge by subtracting the net item value from the minimum order value, AMIW.

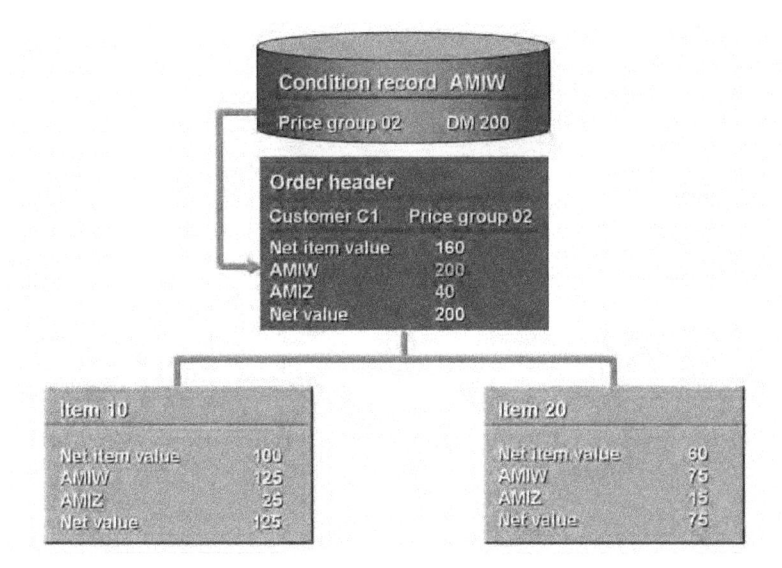

- Condition type PNOO is used to set a manual net price for an item and previous condition records are ignored.
- Condition type PMIN sets a minimum price for an item. Condition type AMIZ is used in conjunction with AMIW.
- AMIZ sets a minimum order price and AMIZ is used to add any surcharge should the order minimum price (AMIW) not be met.

Sales Process

89. Which of the following data is proposed from the customer master when an order is created?
(Only one answer is correct)

(a) Partners
(b) Plant
(c) Payment
(d) All of the above

Answer: d

Explanation:

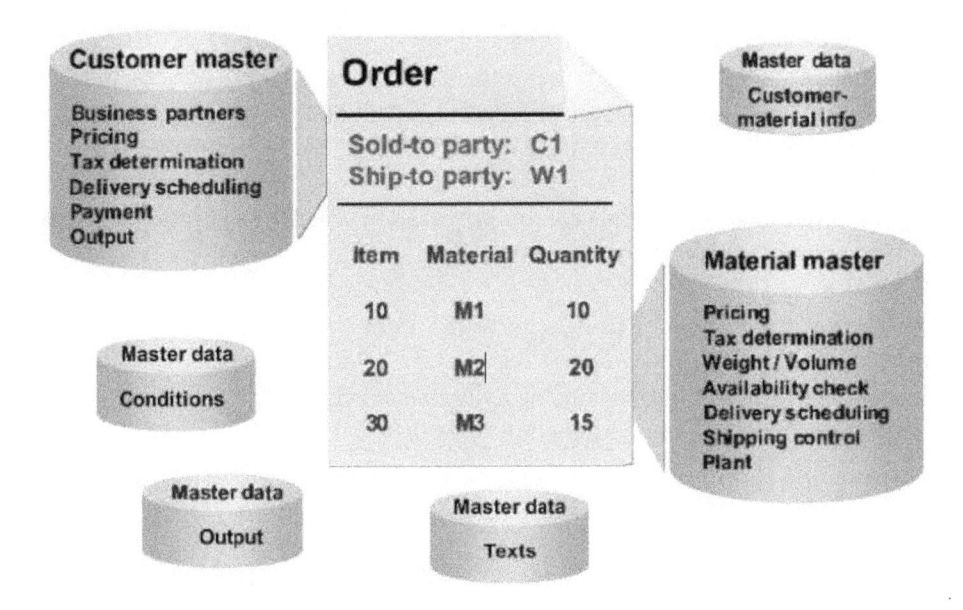

You must store as much data as possible in the master records in the SAP system. This will save your time during order entry and help to avoid incorrect entries.

You can enter different types of master data in the SAP system. For example, you can enter information on business partners, materials, customer-specific materials, item proposals, bills of material (BOMs), prices, discounts and rebates, taxes, freight, output and texts and so on. The system will frequently access the master data during order processing.

In the order overview you can create an order for the company by entering customer-specific material numbers if the customer-specific material information record has already been created.

90. Which of the following data is proposed from the material master when an order is created?
(There are two correct answers to the question)

(a) Partners
(b) Plant
(c) Pricing
(d) Output

Answer: b, c

Explanation:

The system reads the master data that is defined for a customer, a material or a pricing condition. For example, the system reads the specific terms of payment for a customer. The system also reads the sales information from a material master. This information can serve as the source for the delivering plant.

Output related data is part of the Customer Master & not the material master; same is the case with Customer specific material numbers and descriptions

Partner's related data is maintained in customer master. Only Plant and pricing can be proposed from material master when an order is created.

91. To satisfy a customer order, materials can be procured in which of the following ways? (There are three correct answers to the question)

    (a) Replenishment from a vendor using a purchase order
    (b) Issuing directly from stock
    (c) Replenishment from a competitor using a purchase order
    (d) Replenishment from in-house production

Answer: a, b, d

Explanation:

Satisfying an order using existing stock, buying from a vendor or producing in a manufacturing process are all possible in SAP ERP. Buying from a competitor is not sensible.

The way in which a material is obtained for a customer order can depend on the material itself as well as on the sales transaction.

The procurement can, for example:

- result from available stock
- be guaranteed by replenishment (purchase requisition or purchase order, planned order or production order, for example)
- trigger a make-to-order production
- order the outbound delivery via external suppliers (third-party business transaction)
- organize the outbound delivery via another warehouse (stock transfer)

92. To combine multiple orders into single deliveries, which of the following must be the same?
(There are two correct answers to the question)

    (a) Due date for the delivery
    (b) Pallet Size
    (c) Invoice number
    (d) Ship to Address

Answer: a, d

Explanation:

To combine multiple sales orders into a single delivery, the delivery due date, ship-to address and shipping point must be the same.

Outbound deliveries are created for orders that are ready to be shipped. The system copies the relevant data from the order to the outbound delivery.

You can create one or more outbound deliveries from the order. You can also combine items from more than one order in an outbound delivery. To combine them successfully, the orders must correspond with the characteristics that are essential for the shipping process, for example:

- Shipping point
- Due date
- Ship-to address

The system can create deliveries either on-line or as a background job to be executed during off-peak hours.

93. Which of the following information can be stored in a customer material information record?
(There are three correct answers to the question)

    (a) Default delivering plant
    (b) Default order quantity
    (c) Preferred partial delivery indicators
    (d) Customer specific delivery tolerances

Answer: a, c, d

Explanation:

All of the information listed can be stored in a customer material information record except for a default order quantity. Default order quantities are set at material master level.

The customer-material info record is used for storing customer-specific material data. If a customer-material info record has been defined for a customer and a material, the default values take priority over the values in the customer or material master when a document is processed (order, delivery, and so on).

You can use the customer-material information record to maintain the following data:

- Cross-reference from your customer's material number to your material number and the customer's material description.
- Specific shipping information for this customer and material (such as delivery tolerances, specifying if the customer will accept partial deliveries or the default delivering plant).

94. Which of the following are examples of work lists used in sales and distribution? (There are three correct answers to the question)

    (a) Outbound deliveries created with reference to sales orders
    (b) Sales orders that can be created with reference to purchase orders
    (c) Goods issues that can be created with reference to outbound deliveries
    (d) Transfer orders that can be created with reference to outbound deliveries

Answer: a, c, d

Explanation:

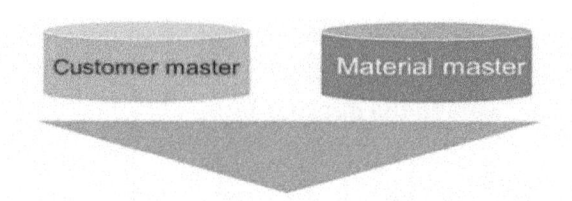

All of the above are work lists used in sales and distribution except for sales orders that can be created with reference to purchase orders. There is no work list function to create sales orders based on purchase orders.

The goods issue can also be posted via collective processing. To do so, select a work list from all the outbound deliveries for which goods issue is ready to be posted and simultaneously post more than one goods issue.

Collective processing can be executed as follows:
- Manually (online)
- Creating a background job (batch) to be executed during off-peak hours

The system controls the posting of the goods issue via the shipping point, the selection date, and other criteria (forwarding agent or route, for example). You receive a list of the deliveries that meet your selection criteria. If necessary, the list can be drilled down to item level. In this list, you can make your selection more precise using sorting and filtering.

Once you have made your selection, post the goods issue.

95. Which of the following partners has been set up in standard order as mandatory partner functions?
    (Only one answer is correct)

    (a) Sold to party
    (b) Bill to party
    (c) Payer
    (d) All of the above

Answer: d

Explanation:

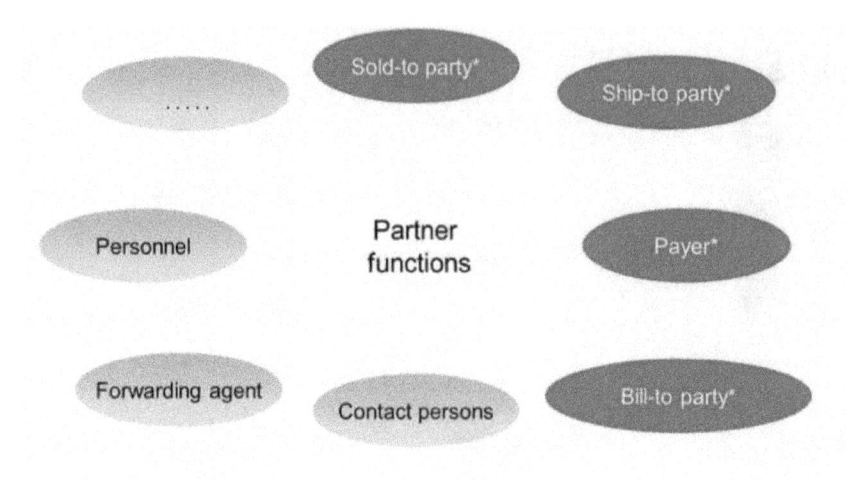

* mandatory functions

You store the partner functions for the customer master in the customer master sales area data. During sales order processing, they are copied as default values into the documents.
For sales order processing, you require the mandatory partner functions sold-to party, ship-to party, payer, and bill-to party. In the course of processing a sales order, they can differ from each other or can be identical.

- Sold-to party: places the order
- Ship-to party: receives goods or services
- Bill-to party: receives the invoice for goods or services
- Payer: is responsible for paying the invoice

Other partner functions, such as contact person or forwarding agent, are not absolutely necessary for sales order processing.

96. **Which of the following is the mandatory sub process of delivery? (There are two correct answers to the question)**

    (a) Creating delivery order
    (b) Picking
    (c) Packing
    (d) Goods Issue

Answer: a, d

Explanation:

Picking & Packing are optional though picking is always used when Warehouse Management is involved.
When the goods issue is posted, the following is carried out automatically:

- The quantity in inventory management and the delivery requirements in materials planning are updated.
- The value change in the balance sheet accounts for inventory accounting is posted (the postings from the relevant accounting document are based on the cost of the material).
- The system creates further documents for Financial Accounting.
- The billing due list is generated.
- The status in all associated sales documents is updated.

97. Which of the following statements are correct regarding billing?
   (There are two correct answers to the question)

   (a) A billing document can be created for either a delivery or a goods issue.
   (b) Billing document consist of a header item and schedule line
   (c) Billing document update status in all relevant sales, delivery and billing documents
   (d) Billing document updates SIS

Answer: c, d

Explanation:
When you save the billing document, the system automatically generates all the required documents for accounting. The system carries out a debit posting in accounting on the customer receivables account and a credit posting on the revenue account.

The accounting document identifies all the subsequent postings in financial accounting that refer back to pricing in SD, such as the receivable on customer accounts or the obtained net sales and taxes on the relevant G/L accounts.

When you save the billing document, the system can automatically generate further documents for Financial Accounting (for the Controlling components as well as for profitability analysis, for example).

The following also occurs when the billing document is posted:

- The status in all related sales, delivery, and billing documents is updated
- The sales statistics in the sales information system are updated
- The data regarding the consumption of the customer's credit limit is updated

Goods issue can happen outside of an SD delivery as well. The billing document is not related to the goods issue but to the delivery.

Billing documents have only header and Item levels and not schedule lines.

Shipping Process and Customizing

98. Which of the following is the delivery type for creating a delivery without reference to a sales order?
(Only one answer is correct)

(a) LF
(b) LO
(c) LR
(d) NL

Answer: b

Explanation:

The screenshot below shows some features of delivery type LO which is the delivery type used for creating a delivery without reference to a sales order.

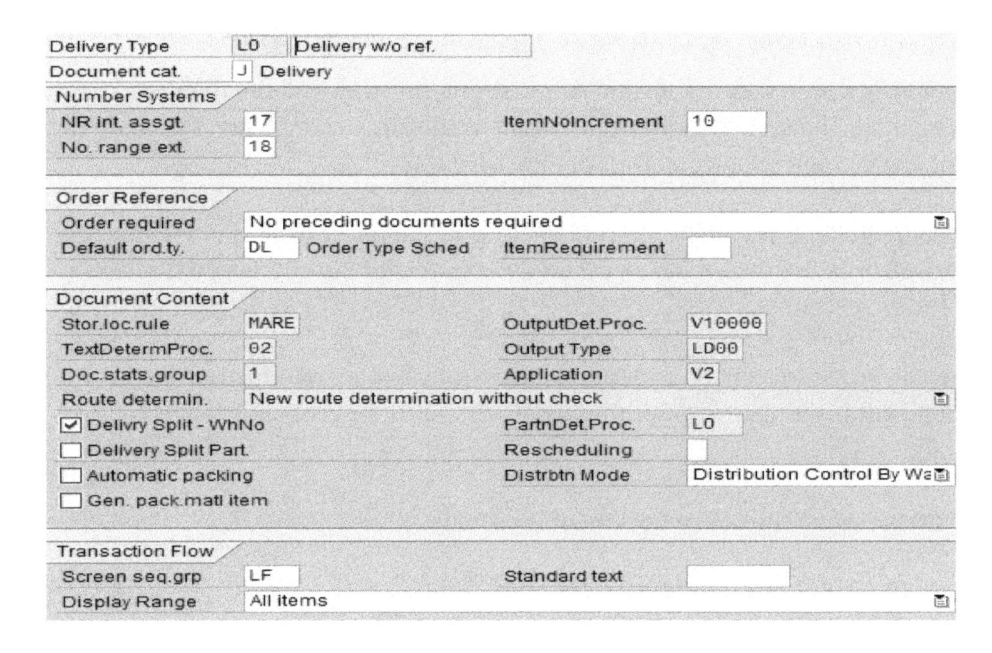

The delivery type controls the entire delivery. You see the delivery type in the delivery header. The delivery types take into account the various business transactions in shipping and goods receipt processing. The delivery types defined in the standard system include:

- **EL**: Inbound delivery (shipping notification)
- **LB**: Delivery for subcontract order
- **LF**: Outbound delivery
- **LO**: Delivery without reference (no sales order necessary in order to create a delivery)
- **LP**: Delivery from project
- **RE**: Returns delivery
- **NL**: Replenishment delivery

99. Which of the following are controlled by the delivery document type?
   (There are three correct answers to the question)

   (a) Number assignment, Output and Texts
   (b) Picking and Packing relevance
   (c) Reference to order
   (d) Shipping (Shipment) relevance

Answer: a, c, d

Explanation:

Number assignment, output and texts along with Reference to order and Shipping relevance are controlled by the delivery document type.

The delivery type controls the delivery document. The delivery type is located in the header of the delivery document. The delivery type of the delivery document is usually generated from the order type of the order to be delivered. In the transaction "Create Outbound Delivery", you can define another delivery type for the delivery document. To use a delivery type within the order-related outbound delivery, the copy control must link the relevant order type to the required delivery types.

To deliver order items, these must be relevant for delivery.
For text and value items, the delivery relevance is defined for the order item category.
For normal items, the delivery relevance is controlled at the level of the schedule line.

In addition, you can define a movement type only for the schedule line category and this creates a connection to Inventory Management. As a result of this, schedule lines are permitted for standard items and the automatic determination of the schedule line category is configured

100. Which of the following are the controlled by the delivery item category?
   (Only one answer is correct)

   (a) Picking and Packing relevance
   (b) Automatic batch determination
   (c) Picking location determination and availability check
   (d) All of the above

Answer: d

Explanation:

Number assignment, Output and Shipping relevance are not controlled by the delivery item category. As soon as you enter an item in the delivery without order reference, the system uses the item category determination to determine the item category for this item.

There must always be a corresponding order item category for this delivery item category. This order item category decides whether this operation is relevant for billing and which billing procedure to use. To create a connection to Inventor Management for the delivery item, the system must allow schedule lines for the order item category.

You can then use the schedule line category determination to determine a schedule line in the order. The movement type that is defined there controls the goods issue posting of the delivery item.

Item Category	C1DG	Del.full Pr.MW free
Document cat.	µ	Delivery

Material/Statistics
- [✓] Mat.no.'0' allowed
- ItemCat.stat.group
- Stk determ.rule

Quantity
- Check quantity 0
- Check minimum qty — A — Note about the situation
- Check overdelivery — A — Note about the situation
- AvailCkOff
- Roundng

Warehouse Control and Packing
- [ ] Relevant for picking
- [✓] StLocation required
- [✓] Determine SLoc
- [ ] Don't chk st. loc.
- [ ] No batch check
- [ ] AutoBatchDeterm
- [ ] Packing control
- [ ] Pack acc. batch itms

Transaction Flow
- TextDetermProcedure
- Standard text

101. **Which of the following is correct regarding picking location determination? (Only one answer is correct)**

   (a) Picking location determination is based on a shipping rule.
   (b) The picking rule "MALA" is based on Shipping point, plant and shipping condition
   (c) The picking location search is activated in the delivery document type.
   (d) None of the above

Answer: b
Explanation:

The following picking rules exist for determining the picking location; you cannot change them in Customizing:

- MALA enables you to determine the picking location according to:
    - ✓ Storage condition
    - ✓ Delivering plant of the delivery item
    - ✓ Shipping point of the delivery

- RETA enables you to determine the picking location according to:

- ✓ Storage location
- ✓ Delivering plant of the delivery item

You set up these rule in plant master control (Logistics - General) in Maintain plants.

102. Which of the following statements are correct regarding batches?
(There are two correct answers to the question)

(a) In order time, a batch can be determined based on various characteristics.
(b) Only one batch can be entered for each delivery item.
(c) It is possible to enter multiple batches for one item on the delivery.
(d) For each delivery item multiple batches are required

Answer: a, c

Explanation:

The Process works as follows:

- A sales order for a material subject to handling in batches is created.
- You run a batch determination, as well as a batch availability and usability check in the sales order. The system determines that the sales order cannot be met with the present stock; a requirement is transferred to production.
- During delivery, batch determination is conducted with reference to the sales order.
- During batch determination, an availability check is carried out.
- Using the inspection results for quality management, inspection certificates can be automatically created

103. Which of the following are mandatory steps in the shipping process?
(There are two correct answers to the question)

(a) Delivery
(b) Picking
(c) Packing
(d) Goods Issue

Answer: a, d

Explanation:

The picking process involves taking goods from a storage location and staging the right quantity in a picking area where the goods will be prepared for shipping, this step is not mandatory.
Packing is used only when materials need to be physically packed and you managed packaging materials.
Billing is optional in the sense you might have a Free of Charge delivery.

104. Which of the following delivery document refers to a sales document?

(Only one answer is correct)

(a) Inbound delivery
(b) Outbound delivery
(c) Transfer delivery
(d) Posting change

Answer: b

Explanation:

Outbound deliveries can be created with reference to a sales document. Inbound deliveries are normally created for purchase orders and stock transport orders. Transfer deliveries do not exist in the standard SAP system. A posting change is normally associated with making adjustments in the financial system and these documents are not delivery related.

105. A shipping point may also be set as the following which means it can be also be used for inbound deliveries?
(Only one answer is correct)

(a) Goods receipt point
(b) Loading point
(c) Company Code
(d) Plant

Answer: a

Explanation:

Shipping points can also be used to represent a goods receipt point for inbound deliveries. A loading point can't be assigned as a shipping point because loading points are dependent upon a shipping point. Shipping points are plant dependent; therefore, they cannot be used to represent a company code. Shipping points are dependent upon a plant; therefore, a shipping point would not be representing a plant.

106. Which of the following information includes the transfer order?
(Only one answer is correct)

(a) Material Number
(b) Quantity to be moved
(c) Source and destination storage bin numbers
(d) All of the above

Answer: d

Explanation:

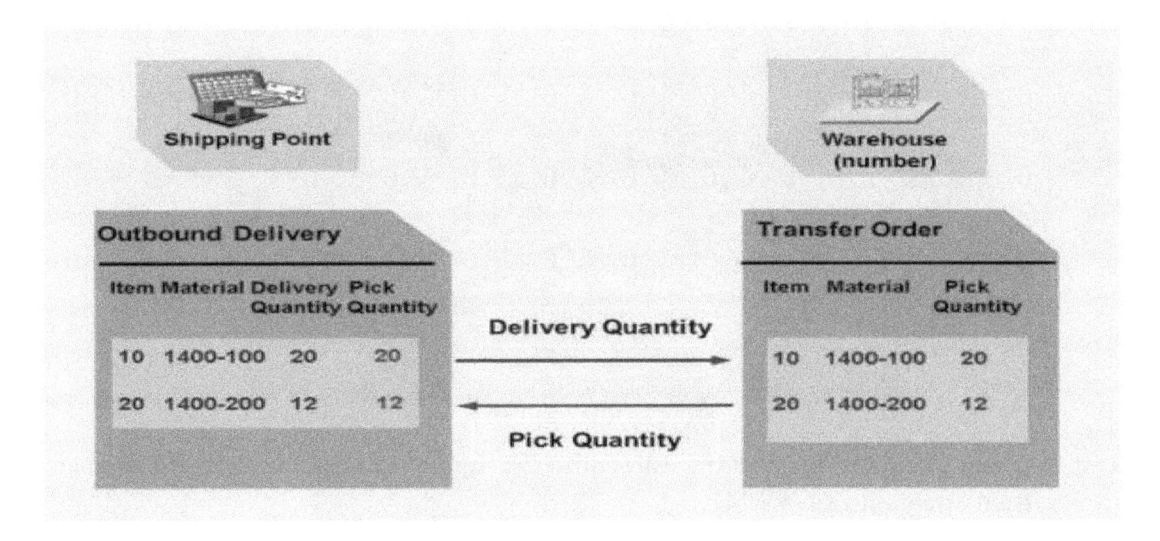

A Transfer Order is an instruction to move materials from a source storage bin to a destination storage bin within a warehouse complex.

TOs include the following information:

- Material number
- Quantity to be moved
- Source and destination storage bin numbers

When you create the TO, the system automatically copies the delivery quantity from the outbound delivery as the picking quantity for them TO. The system automatically enters the picking quantity in the outbound delivery. In Lean WM, the picking quantity is initially the same as the delivery quantity.

107. **Which of the following are required at least for a Lean Warehouse model? (There are two correct answers to the question)**

    (a) Warehouse number
    (b) Storage Type
    (c) Material Number
    (d) Sales document

Answer: a, b

Explanation:

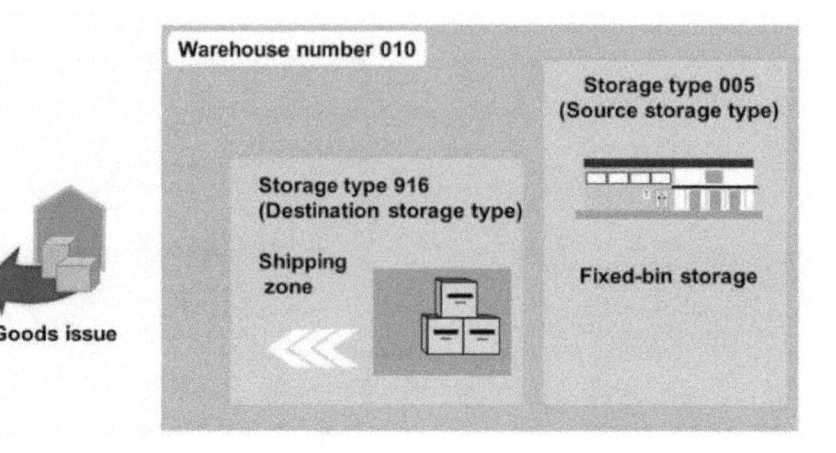

The figure shows a possible model of the warehouse structure of a fixed-bin storage method in the SAP system when using Lean WM.

For Lean WM. you need at least one warehouse number and at least one storage type from which picking takes place. You also need one storage type in which you stage the goods (for example, picking storage type as source storage type and shipping zone as destination storage type).

In the picking area, you can group together storage bins from the stock removal perspective (for example, to distribute the workload evenly). In addition to the picking area, there are other organizational units in the warehouse. These are the staging areas and the doors. They are defined in the outbound delivery or determined by the system, and can also be printed on the picking documents.

You can activate WM in Customizing at the warehouse number level by assigning a warehouse number to a combination of plant and storage type. In this way, the organizational units in the warehouse are linked to inventory management. Also, through this assignment, a status for WM activities is assigned to the respective items in the outbound delivery.

Availability Check

108. Which of the following statements are true about backorder processing?
(Only one answer is correct)

(a) An order can be back-dated if the quantity of an order is not totally confirmed
(b) An order can be back-dated if the delivery date for an order item cannot be kept
(c) Back orders can be processed manually or automatically via rescheduling
(d) All of the above

Answer: d

Explanation:

Backorder Processing

An order item is backdated if:
- the quantity of an order item is not totally confirmed
- the required delivery date for an order item cannot be kept

⬇

Backorder processing

There are two types of backorder processing:

Manual with backorder processing
You can use backorder processing to list sales documents for materials and to process them manually with reference to the confirmation. This means that ATP quantities can be reassigned and any shortfall can be cleared.

Via rescheduling
You can use the delivery priority (proposed from the customer master record for the sales order) as a sorting criterion in automatic rescheduling.

109. In which of the following conditions availability check is carried out during sales order processing?

(There are two correct answers to the question)

(a) Material requires an availability check
(b) Warehouse order is getting expired
(c) Customized the availability check in the transaction
(d) Delivery date of material is completed

Answer: a, b c

Explanation:

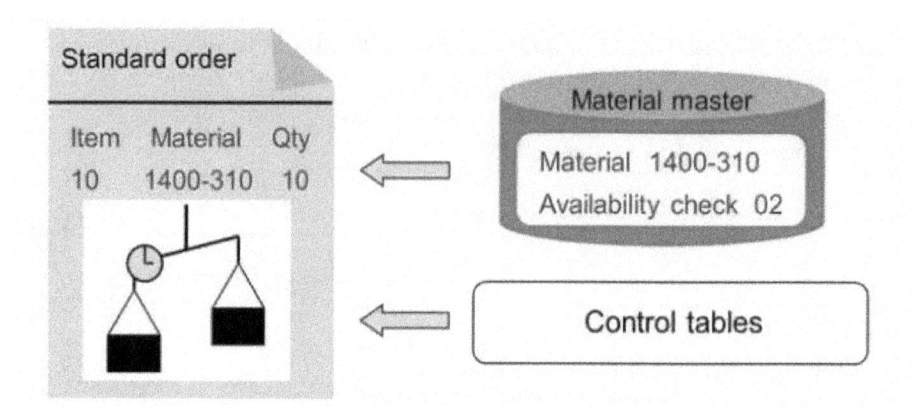

An availability check is carried out during sales order processing if

- The material requires an availability check
- The availability check is set in customizing for this transaction

On the Sales and Distribution tab page in the material master you can: enter in Gen/Plant in the availability check field, which and/or what type of availability check should be carried out for this material during order processing.

There are also various settings in customizing that influence the process flow of the availability check.

110. Shipment scheduling take into consideration certain lead times. Which of the following is incorrect?
    (There are two correct answers to the question)

    (a) Transit time
    (b) Pick and packing time as well as loading time
    (c) Confirmed delivery time
    (d) Billing time

Answer: c, d

Explanation:

There are two different types of scheduling:

Delivery scheduling: The SAP System takes into account the pick/pack time and loading time for a transaction. You define the type of delivery scheduling for each shipping point.

Transportation scheduling: The SAP System takes into account the transit time and the transportation scheduling time for a transaction. You define the type of transportation scheduling on the basis of the route.

111. **At which level, material availability checks in sales order will be performed? (Only one answer is correct)**

(a) Organization level
(b) Plant level
(c) Meta data level
(d) All of the above

Answer: b

Explanation:

Using delivery and transportation scheduling (calculating backwards from the customer's required delivery date) the system calculates several dates for each item in the sales order.

The relevant date for the availability check is the material availability date. On this date enough material has to be available in stock to meet the confirmed customer delivery date.

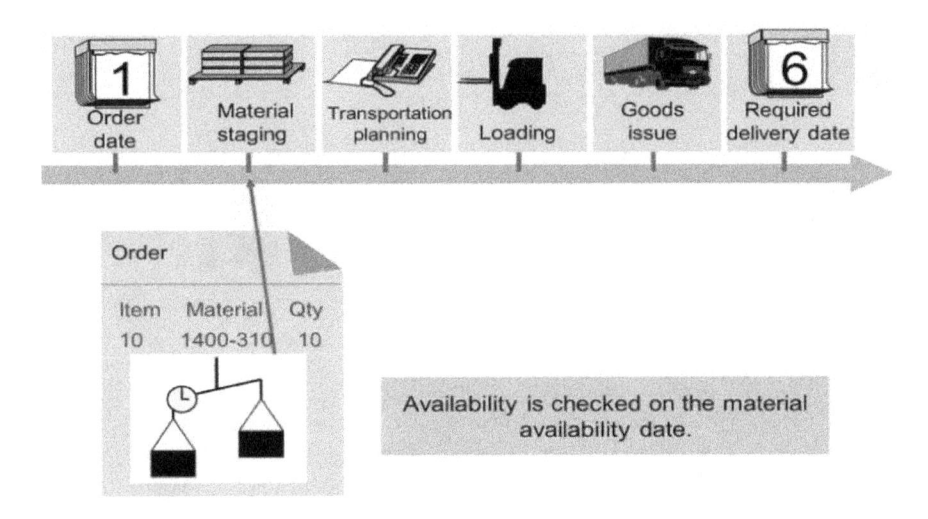

The material availability check in sales orders is performed at plant level for the corresponding item. The plant can be determined automatically or maintained manually. During automatic determination the system looks for a valid default value for the plant in the relevant master data using the following sequence:

1. Customer-material info record
2. Ship-to party customer master record

3. Material master record

112. Which of the following options for partial deliveries on item level exist?
(Only one answer is correct)

(a) Partial delivery is allowed
(b) One delivery has to be created
(c) One complete delivery allowed
(d) All of the above

Answer: d

Explanation:

Complete and Partial Deliveries
You can make agreements with your customers concerning the creation of deliveries. To be more precise: Some customers might always want you to make one complete delivery (all order items have to be delivered in full), while others might allow partial deliveries (for example if a single item cannot be confirmed for the requested delivery date).

You can maintain the corresponding parameter for each sales area in the customer master data. If partial deliveries are basically allowed by the customer, you can also determine whether a partial delivery of a single item is possible.

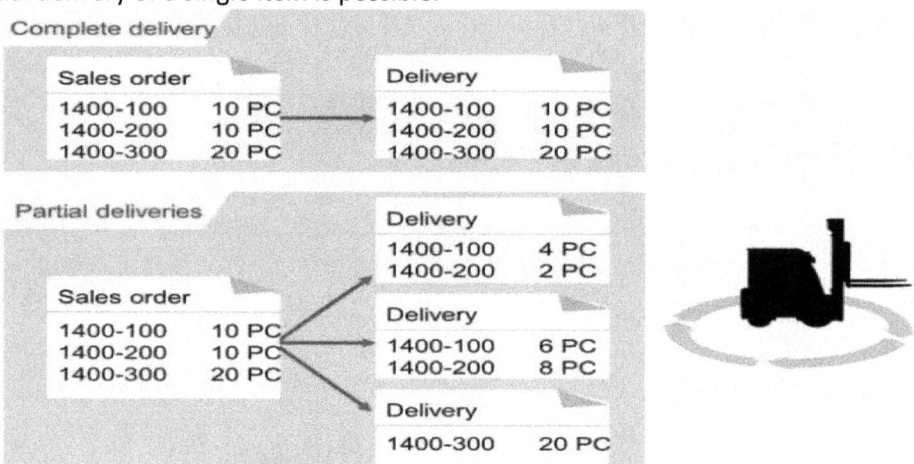

Complete delivery

Sales order		Delivery	
1400-100	10 PC	1400-100	10 PC
1400-200	10 PC	1400-200	10 PC
1400-300	20 PC	1400-300	20 PC

Partial deliveries

Delivery	
1400-100	4 PC
1400-200	2 PC

Sales order		Delivery	
1400-100	10 PC	1400-100	6 PC
1400-200	10 PC	1400-200	8 PC
1400-300	20 PC		

Delivery	
1400-300	20 PC

The following options for partial deliveries on item level exist:

- Partial delivery is allowed
- One delivery with quantity greater than zero has to be created
- One delivery (also with quantity = 0) has to be created
- Only complete delivery (per item) allowed
- No limit to subsequent deliveries

113. Which of the following is a pre requisite for the availability check in the sales order?
(Only one answer is correct)

(a) Delivery scheduling completion
(b) Material availability
(c) Delivery item availability
(d) Partial delivery has to be completed

Answer: a

Explanation:

The availability checks take place on the material availability date. The materials are required on this date, so that enough time remains for picking, loading and transportation before the required delivery date.
This means the availability date must be determined in the sales order before the availability check is carried out.

114. **Which of the following statements are true about routes?**
     (There are three correct answers to the question)

    (a) They are made up of itineraries and shipping types.
    (b) They consist of connection points in which only legs can connect the points.
    (c) The volume of the items in the delivery is considered when determining a route in the delivery.
    (d) The shipping point, ship-to, sold-to, and material are factors in determining the proposed route.

Answer: b, c, d

Explanation:

Routes are determined depending on the following criteria:

- Country and departure zone (departure zone of the shipping point)
- Shipping conditions agreed in the sales order
- The shipping condition is defined in shipping point determination.
- Transportation group of the material
- Country and transportation zone (receiving zone) of the ship-to party

The SAP System copies the route from the sales document item into the delivery at header level. To define route determination, you must edit the following points:

- Define transportation zones for each country. These transportation zones can be either departure zones for the shipping point or receiving zones for the ship-to party.
- Assign the departure zones to the shipping points.
- Define transportation groups for the materials.
- Specify the routes to be selected according to the given criteria in sales processing.

- Define the delivery types for which route determination should be repeated and set the necessary indicator in the appropriate delivery types.
- Define the weight groups.

Route determination can be repeated by the SAP System when creating a delivery.

Delivery types, for which route determination is to be repeated, should be marked as such in their definition. In this case, route determination is carried out depending on weight. The route applies to the entire delivery

Organizational Structures

115. Which of the following are organizational elements for sales and distribution?
(There are two correct answers to the question)

(a) Company Code
(b) Sales organization
(c) Controlling Area
(d) Purchasing organization

Answer: a, b

Explanation:

In sales and distribution, the relevant organizational elements are company code and Sales organization. Controlling Area represents organizational elements in controlling (CO).
A purchasing organization is an organizational element in the procure to pay business process.

- Company code
- Sales area
    - Sales organization
    - Distribution channel
    - Division
- Plant
- Storage location
- Shipping point

116. Which of the following is the smallest organizational unit of financial accounting?
(Only one answer is correct)

(a) Company code
(b) Sales Area
(c) Plant
(d) Storage Location

Answer: a

Explanation:

A company code is the smallest organizational unit of Financial Accounting for which a complete, self-contained set of accounts can be drawn up for purposes of external accounting.

This includes recording all the relevant transactions and generating all the supporting documents required for financial statements. A company code can represent a company within a corporate group or a subsidiary for example.

The company code is relevant for sales and distribution processes since the revenues of the sales department have to be assigned to it.

The following figure lists some key facts about the company code as an organizational unit.

- Legal entity and independent accounting unit
- At company code level, you create:
    → balance sheets required by law
    → profit and loss statement

117. Which of the following characterizes the way in which goods and services are distributed?

(Only one answer is correct)

(a) Sales organization
(b) Distribution Channel
(c) Company code
(d) Shipping Point

Answer: b

Explanation:

The distribution channel characterizes the way in which goods and services are distributed. Distribution channels have to be assigned to at least one sales organization (multiple assignments are possible).

To use the sales and distribution functions you need to define at least one distribution channel in the system.

You can use different distribution channels to:
- Define responsibilities
- Carry out flexible price structuring
- Differentiate sales statistics

In practice, companies use different distribution channels to separate domestic sales from foreign sales for example or you might use a sales distribution channel (for selling products) and a service distribution channel (for selling maintenance and repair services).

118. Which of the following represents a product line?
    (Only one answer is correct)

    (a) Sales organization
    (b) Division
    (c) Sales Area
    (d) Company code

Answer: b

Explanation:

Materials and services can be grouped using divisions. A division can represent a certain product group. You can therefore restrict price agreements with a customer to a particular division. Statistical analysis can also be conducted by division.

These divisions should be used within your sales structure because some people in your sales department are very familiar with a certain product group (for example tools for metal processing), while others have technical knowledge about a different product group (for example, tools for polymer processing).

Using the corresponding divisions, you can take this into account when setting up your sales structure. Several divisions can be assigned to a sales organization. To use the sales and distribution functions in the system at least one division has to be defined in the system.

The following figure illustrates the relevance of divisions within the organizational structure.

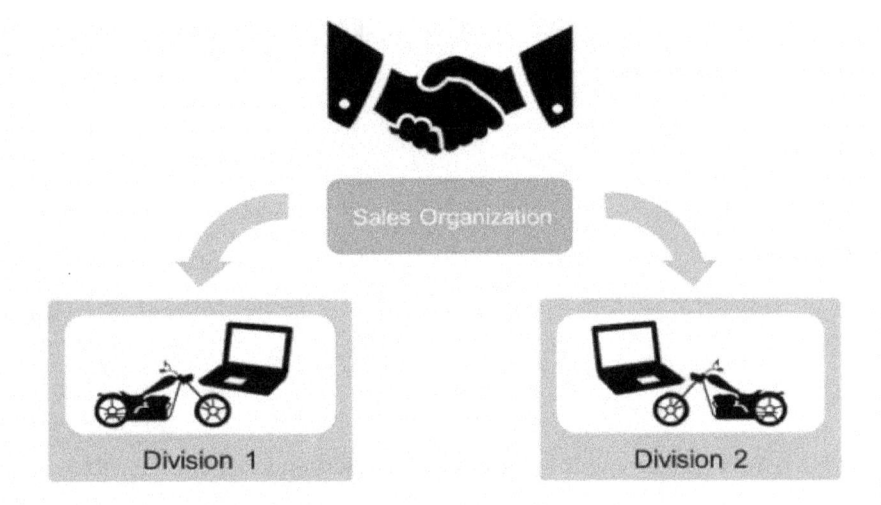

- Represents a product line
- Examples: motorcycles, spare parts, services, and so on

119. Sales area is a combination of the following?
(Only one answer is correct)

    (a) Sales organization
    (b) Distribution Channel
    (c) Division
    (d) All of the above

Answer: d

Explanation:

A sales area is a combination of one sales organization, one distribution channel, and one division. It defines the distribution channel a sales organization uses to sell products from a certain division.

Each sales and distribution document is assigned to exactly one sales area. This assignment cannot be changed. A sales area can belong to only one company code. This relationship is realized by the assignment of the corresponding sales organization to the relevant company code. At least one sales area has to be defined in the system to execute sales and distribution processes.

When processing sales and distribution documents, the system accesses various master data depending on the sales area. This master data includes customer master data, prices, and discounts. The system also performs a number of validity checks on certain entries based on the sales area.

120. Which of the following is essential for determining the shipping point?
(Only one answer is correct)

    (a) Plant
    (b) Sales Area
    (c) Distribution Channel
    (d) All of the above

Answer: a

Explanation:

The following information concerning the usage of plants within sales and distribution processes is important:
- To use the sales and distribution functions in the system you need at least one plant.
- Each plant is uniquely assigned to a company code.
- To use a plant within a sales and distribution process it has to be assigned to at least one combination of a sales organization and a distribution channel. Multiple assignments are possible.
- The plant is essential for determining the shipping point.

121. Which of the following are the prerequisites for Assigning Shipping Points According to Storage Locations?
    (Only one answer is correct)

    (a) You have defined shipping conditions
    (b) You have defined Plant
    (c) You have defined a storage location.
    (d) All of the above

Answer: d

Explanation:

Ensure that the following shipping point assignments are defined in Customizing for Logistics Execution under
Shipping→ Basic Shipping Functions →Shipping Point and Goods Receiving Point Determination →Set Up Storage-Location-Dependent Shipping Point Determination →Assign Shipping Points according to Storage Location.

122. At the time of order creation, the system determines the required material availability date based on the delivery date requested by the customer. This scheduling takes into account following times?
    (Only one answer is correct)

    (a) Transit time: Time required to ship an outbound delivery to the ship-to party
    (b) Loading time: Time required for loading the goods.
    (c) Pick/pack time: Time required for picking, packing, and so on
    (d) All of the above

Answer: d

Explanation:

When you create an order, the system can determine the required material availability date based on the delivery date requested by the customer. The goods to be delivered must be available for shipping at this point in time.

Scheduling takes into account the following times:

- Transit time: Time required to ship an outbound delivery to the ship-to party
- Loading time: Time required for loading the goods.
- Pick/pack time: Time required for picking, packing, and so on
- Transportation lead time: Time required for organizing the transportation.

The loading time and pick/pack time come from the shipping point; the transit time and the transportation planning time come from the route.

123. For Delivery Item Category, if "Relevant for picking" is not activated then which of the following is correct?
(Only one answer is correct)

(a) Transfer Order is not required
(b) Transfer Order is mandatory
(c) Material is not relevant for delivery
(d) None of the above

Answer: a

Explanation:

In the case of outbound deliveries, only the delivery items that are relevant for picking are transferred to the Warehouse Management (WM) component. Certain items such as text items or service items (consulting activities) are not relevant for picking.

In the case of inbound deliveries, this indicator controls whether the item is relevant for put away. This indicator must be set in order for the item to be included in a Warehouse Management transfer order and then put away.

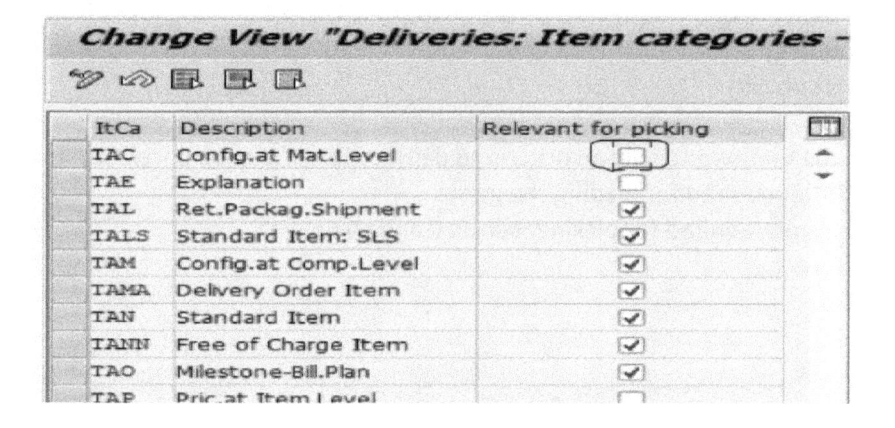

Cross functional Customizing

124. Which of the following requirements to be met before data is copied from a referenced document?
   (There are three correct answers to the question)

   (a) Does the copied and referenced document have the same ship to parties
   (b) Was the item being copied, rejected?
   (c) Have the items being copied already been referenced
   (d) Has a validity period of the referenced document been exceeded?

Answer: b, c, d

Explanation:

Copy Control Tasks and Process

The system allows for ship to parties to be different in case before data is copied from a reference document.

The copying control tables are an important element in Customizing for your SAP system.

- These tables control many of the functions that are executed when you create a document that references a preceding document.

Before the data is copied, the system can check whether certain requirements have been met. Examples of these requirements are:

- Do the reference document and copied document have the same sold-to party?
- Was the item being copied rejected?
- Have the items being copied already been referenced?
- Has the validity period of the reference document been exceeded?

You can control which data should be copied when referencing, such as header data, partner data or conditions.

The "Create with Reference" function is available on the initial entry screen as well as during document entry so that you could, for example, combine several quotations for one customer in one sales order.

125. Which of the following are the incorrect statements regarding texts that are maintained in the area of sales and distribution?
   (There are two correct answers to the question)

   (a) Customer master for financial texts, Sales & Distribution texts and Contact person
   (b) Customer master: only for Sales & distribution texts

(c) Material master
(d) In documents only at header level

Answer: b, d

Explanation:

Text can be maintained at customer master: only for S & D texts and in documents at header level.
You must carry out the following steps:

- Select a text object and define the rules for text determination for this object. Text objects are, for example, the sales texts in the customer master record or the sales document header.
- Define the access sequences. This way, you define how the SAP System should determine the texts for a text type.
- Group the text types together in text determination procedures. The SAP System then proposes the text types from the procedure when you maintain a customer master record or a sales & distribution document. The search for the respective text is carried out using the access sequence which you have stored for each text type in the procedure.

Allocate the text determination procedures so that a procedure applies to the following criteria in each case:
- Account group customer
- sales & distribution document type
- item category

The following text objects exist:

- Customer
- central texts
- accounting texts
- texts concerning the contact persons
- sales and distribution texts
- sales document
- header texts
- item texts
- delivery
- header texts
- item texts
- billing document
- header texts
- item texts
- CAS

126. **Which of the following is the transmission medium for SAP?**
    (Only one answer is correct)

    (a) Printer
    (b) Telex / telefax
    (c) Externaltransmission
    (d) All of the above

Answer : d

Explanation:

All the above can be used for transmission of information.

Sales and distribution output can be sent both electronically and by mail. Output control which is dependent on various criteria allows output to be processed and sent subject to certain conditions and restrictions.

You have to define the following:

- Rules of output determination
- Print parameters
- When the sending of output is to be initiated

127. **Which of the following options can be customized in the copying control at the item level?**
    (There are three correct answers to the question)

    (a) Copying Requirements
    (b) Data Transfer Routines
    (c) Availability check control
    (d) Plant and organization level maintenance

Answer: a, b, c

Explanation:

Copy Control on Item Level

[Diagram showing copying control settings with Target sales document type OR - Standard order, Source sales document type QT - Quotation, Item category AGN - Standard item, and various field entries including VBAP 051 General item, VBKD 101 Compl. bus. data item, VBPA 001 Partner item, FPLA 251 Conditions, Copying req. 301 Item reason for rej., checkboxes for Copy schedule lines, Update document flow, Ind. Do not copy batch, Configuration, Retrigger structure/free goods, and settings for Quant/value pos/neg +, Copy quantity, Pricing type A, Value cont. copy mode, Copy product select.]

In copying control, the item level controls are defined for each item category for every "Target document type / Source document type" pairing.

The details screen for an item category contains:
- Copying requirements
- Data transfer routines and includes the following important entries:

• Quantity/value pos/neg:
Controls how the completed quantity in the item in the source document is affected by the copying action.

• Copy quantity:
Determines the quantity that is copied to the target document (for example, blank = best possible quantity = open order quantity for sales document type SP).

• Pricing type:
Specifies how pricing data should be handled when copying.

• Update document flow:
Specifies whether the system updates the document flow when a document is copied.

128. Which of the following statements are true?
    (There are three correct answers to the question)

    (a) You can store texts in the master data and copy them into sales and distribution documents
    (b) You can determine the conditions under which texts are to be copied
    (c) You can copy texts in a single language only
    (d) You can copy a standard text into a sales document

Answer: a, b, d

Explanation:

- Texts can be stored in the master data and copied from master data into sales and distribution documents.
- Texts can also be copied from a reference document to another sales and distribution document, for example, from a quotation to an order or from an order to a delivery document.
- Texts can be copied in a specific language.
- You can determine the conditions under which texts are to be copied, for example, whether the text is copied from the customer master record or from a preceding document.
- You can also copy a standard text into a sales document (for example, Christmas greetings).

129. Which of the following text sources do you access in the material master?
   (There are two correct answers to the question)

   (a) Marketing Notes
   (b) Delivery Text
   (c) Sales Text
   (d) Purchase Order text

Answer: c, d

Explanation:

Sources of Text

Texts are stored in various objects in documents in the SAP system, such as the customer master record, the material master record, the customer-material-info record and in all documents.

The customer master record contains central texts, texts specific to Accounting and to Sales and Distribution as well as texts for contact persons. You can define different text types for each of these areas.

Example of sales-specific text types:

Sales note, marketing note, shipping specification, etc.
The material master record contains a purchase order text and a sales text.
Documents contain texts at header and item level.
You can enter texts in several different languages.

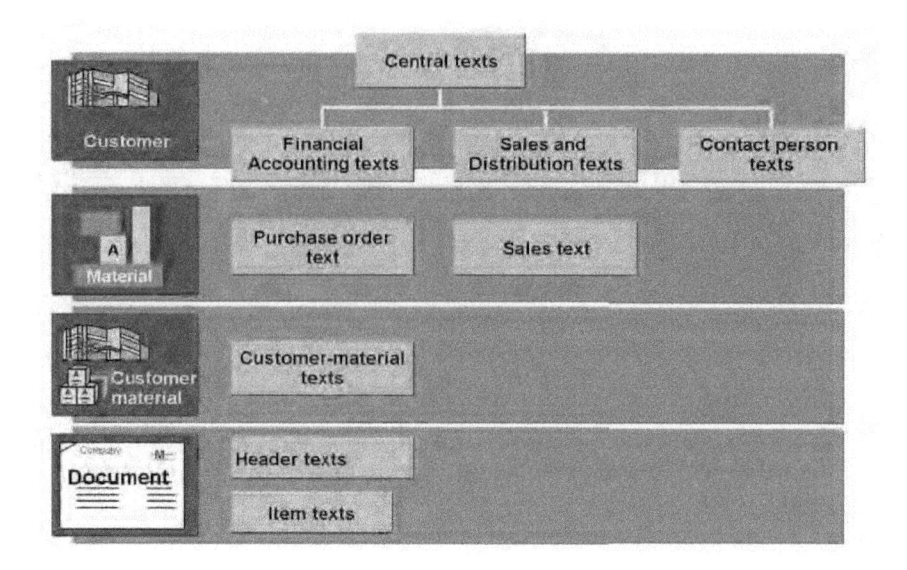

130. Which of the following can you use to view adjustments made in the output determination?
    (Only one answer is correct)

(a) Analysis
(b) Condition record
(c) Create
(d) Change

Answer: a

Explanation:

Output Determination - Analysis

The analysis function can be used to view what output types were determined. Condition records, creating or change do not provide any functions to view an output analysis.

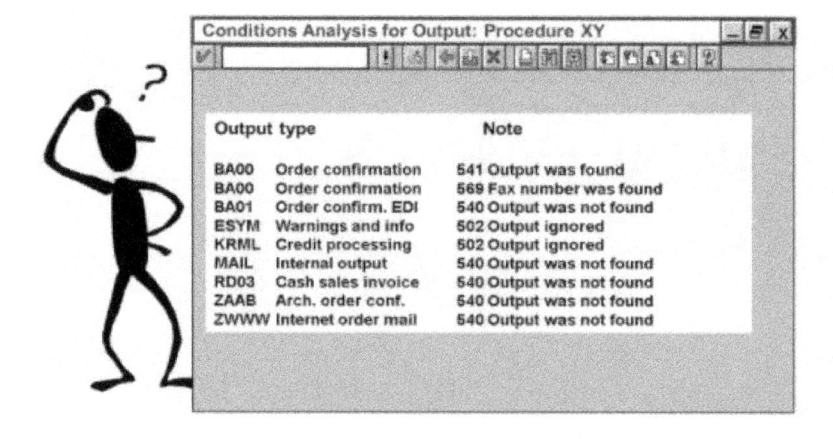

You can use the Analysis function for output determination in the sales document screens (with the create or change functions).

Menu path:
Extras → Output → Header (or item) → Process
Choose Go to → Determination analysis

Master Data

131. Which of the following information can be stored in a customer material information record?
(Only one answer is correct)

(a) Default delivering plant
(b) Customer material number
(c) Customer specific delivery tolerances
(d) All of the above

Answer: d

Explanation:

You can use the customer-material information record to maintain the following data:

- Cross-reference from your customer's material number to your material number and the customer's material description.

- Specific shipping information for this customer and material (such as delivery tolerances, specifying if the customer will accept partial deliveries or the default delivering plant).

132. Which of the following are controlled by the condition type?
(There are three correct answers to the question)

(a) Whether or not scales are allowed
(b) Whether the condition is shown in the pricing analysis screens
(c) Default values for validity periods
(d) Whether the condition is a header or item condition

Answer: a, c, d

Explanation

Condition type customizing controls the use of scales, header or item condition and default values for validity periods. There are no settings controlling the showing of conditions in the pricing analysis screen. The use of a condition type as a numerator or denominator is defined in the formula code and not in the condition type.

133. Which of the following tab pages are used for maintaining the sales area data?
(Only one answer is correct)

(a) Payment transactions
(b) Marketing
(c) Export data

(d) Partner Functions

Answer: d

Explanation:

[Diagram: Customer master Sales area data cylinder showing:]
- **Sales**: Sales office, currency, sales district, price group, ...
- **Shipping**: Shipping condition, delivering plant, transportation zone, ...
- **Billing documents**: Output tax classification, payment condition, ...
- **Partner functions**: Ship-to party, bill-to party, payer, ...

You can maintain the sales area data in various ways, depending on the sales area (sales organization, distribution channel, division).

The following tab pages are used:

- Sales
- Shipping
- Billing documents
- Partner functions

By changing the Customizing settings, you can hide certain fields on a tab page or make them required entry fields

134. Which of the following defines multiple uses of a condition?
(Only one answer is correct)

(a) Condition record
(b) Condition Type
(c) Validity Period
(d) All of the above

Answer: b

Explanation:

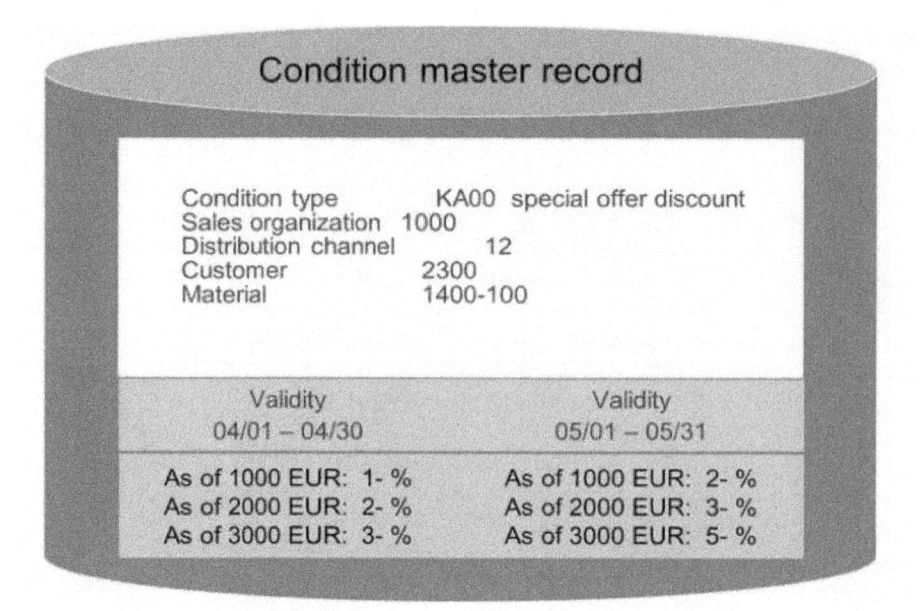

Condition master record

```
Condition type        KA00  special offer discount
Sales organization    1000
Distribution channel       12
Customer              2300
Material              1400-100
```

Validity 04/01 – 04/30	Validity 05/01 – 05/31
As of 1000 EUR: 1- % As of 2000 EUR: 2- % As of 3000 EUR: 3- %	As of 1000 EUR: 2- % As of 2000 EUR: 3- % As of 3000 EUR: 5- %

- The condition master data includes prices, surcharges and discounts, freights, and taxes.
- The condition type defines multiple uses of a condition.
- You can have a percentage, a quantity-dependent, or an amount-dependent surcharge or discount, depending on the condition type.
- By specifying a validity period, you can restrict a price agreement to a certain period.
- You can maintain values within a condition record (price, surcharge, and discount) according to a scale. There is no limit to the number of scale levels.

CPSIA information can be obtained
at www.ICGtesting.com
Printed in the USA
LVHW09s1440310718
585489LV00019B/383/P